How To Live Like A Christian Should

Christian Should

— Daily Nuggets —

Dr. Earl Allen

ISBN-10: 1-878766-97-X
ISBN-13: 978-1-878766-97-7

Miracle Publications International, Inc.
11601 Shadow Creek Parkway, Suite 111 #109
Pearland, Texas 77584
Email: info@drearlallen.com

How To Live Like A Christian Should

Christian Should

— *Daily Nuggets* —

INTRODUCTION

At age nineteen, my friend and I decided to go swimming in the American River in Sacramento, California. Moments later when a speedboat rushed by, it created enormous waves that caused my inner tube to drift out into the middle of the river. After trying many times to retrieve it, I became exhausted! Twice I yelled to my friend to help me, but because he knew I could swim well, he thought I was joking. The third time while I was completely under water, I actually heard a voice say these words to me, *"Earl, you are going to drown unless you do exactly what I tell you to do! I want you to go back up and this time, yell as loud as you can, and as soon as you feel Dave's fingertips touch you, I want you to go completely limp; don't move, just let Dave have complete control."* I did exactly as I was told and the next thing I knew I was on the shore, and Dave was trying to revive me. That day, the difference between life and death was my decision to let go and release all control to someone else.

During this experience, I was not a Christian and knew absolutely nothing about the Holy Spirit. But what I learned was that God was not ready for me to die and that when you listen to and obey the voice of the Holy Spirit that you hear on the inside, you will live and not die!

Since that drowning experience, I have had numerous encounters with the Holy Spirit. One morning while preparing to go to my office, I heard the now-familiar Voice and this time, He gave me some words to write down. He said these words were more valuable than if I had all the money in the world, and He told me to recite them every day! In addition, He (The Holy Spirit) told me to encourage as many people as I could to confess these words on a daily basis. This is the reason that I have repeatedly given a place of prominence to the *Believer's Declaration*. I believe that you will find this statement to be very valuable in your everyday life along with each daily nugget. Sincerely expect the daily nuggets and the Declaration to genuinely help you learn *How to Live Like a Christian Should!*

THE BELIEVER'S DECLARATION OF LIBERATION©

*Thank You, Holy Spirit, for helping
me to release all control to You so that God's
Perfect Will for my life today is done.
In the Name of Jesus. Amen.*

Be a God pleaser and you

won't have time to be a

people pleaser.

⟳DAY⟳
1

THE BELIEVER'S DECLARATION OF LIBERATION©

*Thank You, Holy Spirit, for helping
me to release all control to You so that God's
Perfect Will for my life today is done.
In the Name of Jesus. Amen.*

Do it God's way

and your way won't get

in the way.

DAY
2

THE BELIEVER'S DECLARATION OF LIBERATION©

*Thank You, Holy Spirit, for helping
me to release all control to You so that God's
Perfect Will for my life today is done.
In the Name of Jesus. Amen.*

God's grace is sufficient, and you should believe that your faith in God's grace is sufficient.

DAY
3

THE BELIEVER'S DECLARATION OF LIBERATION©

*Thank You, Holy Spirit, for helping
me to release all control to You so that God's
Perfect Will for my life today is done.
In the Name of Jesus. Amen.*

Believe that God's plans

for your life are better

than your plans for

your life.

THE BELIEVER'S DECLARATION OF LIBERATION©

*Thank You, Holy Spirit, for helping
me to release all control to You so that God's
Perfect Will for my life today is done.
In the Name of Jesus. Amen.*

Don't be too quick to give up on people; God did not give up on you.

⟿DAY⟾
5

THE BELIEVER'S DECLARATION OF LIBERATION©

*Thank You, Holy Spirit, for helping
me to release all control to You so that God's
Perfect Will for my life today is done.
In the Name of Jesus. Amen.*

God expects you to have

big dreams because you are

created in His image.

⟳DAY⟳
6

THE BELIEVER'S DECLARATION OF LIBERATION©

*Thank You, Holy Spirit, for helping
me to release all control to You so that God's
Perfect Will for my life today is done.
In the Name of Jesus. Amen.*

Y ou are either living a

God-centered life or a

self-centered life.

⮞ DAY ⮜
7

THE BELIEVER'S DECLARATION OF LIBERATION©

*Thank You, Holy Spirit, for helping
me to release all control to You so that God's
Perfect Will for my life today is done.
In the Name of Jesus. Amen.*

With the help of the
Holy Spirit, you can do
whatever God wants
you to do.

⌒DAY⌒
8

THE BELIEVER'S DECLARATION OF LIBERATION©

*Thank You, Holy Spirit, for helping
me to release all control to You so that God's
Perfect Will for my life today is done.
In the Name of Jesus. Amen.*

God never sleeps, but

He watches over you while

you sleep.

⟶ DAY ⟵
9

THE BELIEVER'S DECLARATION OF LIBERATION©

*Thank You, Holy Spirit, for helping
me to release all control to You so that God's
Perfect Will for my life today is done.
In the Name of Jesus. Amen.*

Don't expect God to

bless what you have started

if you didn't ask Him to

bless it before you started.

THE BELIEVER'S DECLARATION OF LIBERATION©

*Thank You, Holy Spirit, for helping
me to release all control to You so that God's
Perfect Will for my life today is done.
In the Name of Jesus. Amen.*

If you keep looking for

the good in others,

you'll find it.

⟞DAY⟝
11

THE BELIEVER'S DECLARATION OF LIBERATION©

*Thank You, Holy Spirit, for helping
me to release all control to You so that God's
Perfect Will for my life today is done.
In the Name of Jesus. Amen.*

When you talk about Jesus, you are talking about God.

⟶ DAY ⟵
12

THE BELIEVER'S DECLARATION OF LIBERATION©

*Thank You, Holy Spirit, for helping
me to release all control to You so that God's
Perfect Will for my life today is done.
In the Name of Jesus. Amen.*

When you have an opportunity to express love to somebody, don't talk yourself out of it.

⤙DAY⤚
13

THE BELIEVER'S DECLARATION OF LIBERATION©

*Thank You, Holy Spirit, for helping
me to release all control to You so that God's
Perfect Will for my life today is done.
In the Name of Jesus. Amen.*

I f you have not read your

Bible today, thank God

you still have time.

⟿DAY⟿
14

THE BELIEVER'S DECLARATION OF LIBERATION©

*Thank You, Holy Spirit, for helping
me to release all control to You so that God's
Perfect Will for my life today is done.
In the Name of Jesus. Amen.*

Y ou may not get to the

top, but God doesn't want

you to stay at the bottom.

⬠DAY⬠
15

THE BELIEVER'S DECLARATION OF LIBERATION©

*Thank You, Holy Spirit, for helping
me to release all control to You so that God's
Perfect Will for my life today is done.
In the Name of Jesus. Amen.*

G od doesn't create

failures; you must learn to

be a failure.

⟿ DAY ⟿
16

THE BELIEVER'S DECLARATION OF LIBERATION©

*Thank You, Holy Spirit, for helping
me to release all control to You so that God's
Perfect Will for my life today is done.
In the Name of Jesus. Amen.*

When you need help,
don't be too proud to
accept the help God
sends you.

⸺DAY⸺
17

THE BELIEVER'S DECLARATION OF LIBERATION©

*Thank You, Holy Spirit, for helping
me to release all control to You so that God's
Perfect Will for my life today is done.
In the Name of Jesus. Amen.*

Keep looking for what

God promised you, and

you'll know it when

it comes.

⊸DAY⊸
18

THE BELIEVER'S DECLARATION OF LIBERATION©

*Thank You, Holy Spirit, for helping
me to release all control to You so that God's
Perfect Will for my life today is done.
In the Name of Jesus. Amen.*

Y ou won't pray an

unanswerable prayer if you

ask the Holy Spirit to

help you.

⟶ DAY ⟵
19

THE BELIEVER'S DECLARATION OF LIBERATION©

*Thank You, Holy Spirit, for helping
me to release all control to You so that God's
Perfect Will for my life today is done.
In the Name of Jesus. Amen.*

Expect more from God

when you believe that

you'll get more.

THE BELIEVER'S DECLARATION OF LIBERATION©

*Thank You, Holy Spirit, for helping
me to release all control to You so that God's
Perfect Will for my life today is done.
In the Name of Jesus. Amen.*

Citizenship in God's

Kingdom is available to

anyone who accepts Jesus.

THE BELIEVER'S DECLARATION OF LIBERATION©

*Thank You, Holy Spirit, for helping
me to release all control to You so that God's
Perfect Will for my life today is done.
In the Name of Jesus. Amen.*

Y ou'll never regret doing

what God wants you to do when

He wants you to do it.

⟜ DAY ⟜
22

THE BELIEVER'S DECLARATION OF LIBERATION©

Thank You, Holy Spirit, for helping
me to release all control to You so that God's
Perfect Will for my life today is done.
In the Name of Jesus. Amen.

When you are talking about the Holy Spirit, you are talking about God.

DAY
23

THE BELIEVER'S DECLARATION OF LIBERATION©

*Thank You, Holy Spirit, for helping
me to release all control to You so that God's
Perfect Will for my life today is done.
In the Name of Jesus. Amen.*

Give God what you promised Him, and He will give you what He promised you.

THE BELIEVER'S DECLARATION OF LIBERATION©

*Thank You, Holy Spirit, for helping
me to release all control to You so that God's
Perfect Will for my life today is done.
In the Name of Jesus. Amen.*

Today is not the same as yesterday, but Jesus is the same every day.

~DAY~
25

THE BELIEVER'S DECLARATION OF LIBERATION©

Thank You, Holy Spirit, for helping me to release all control to You so that God's Perfect Will for my life today is done. In the Name of Jesus. Amen.

There are two sides to every story unless God is telling the story.

THE BELIEVER'S DECLARATION OF LIBERATION©

*Thank You, Holy Spirit, for helping
me to release all control to You so that God's
Perfect Will for my life today is done.
In the Name of Jesus. Amen.*

Stop expecting God to be

fooled by your schemes.

~DAY~
27

THE BELIEVER'S DECLARATION OF LIBERATION©

*Thank You, Holy Spirit, for helping
me to release all control to You so that God's
Perfect Will for my life today is done.
In the Name of Jesus. Amen.*

Your life will be what
God wants it to be if you
keep Him in your life.

THE BELIEVER'S DECLARATION OF LIBERATION©

*Thank You, Holy Spirit, for helping
me to release all control to You so that God's
Perfect Will for my life today is done.
In the Name of Jesus. Amen.*

As often as possible,

remind yourself of what

God has done for you and

how He has kept

His promises.

⊸DAY⊸
29

THE BELIEVER'S DECLARATION
OF LIBERATION©

*Thank You, Holy Spirit, for helping
me to release all control to You so that God's
Perfect Will for my life today is done.
In the Name of Jesus. Amen.*

Remember, because

of Jesus, your sins have

been forgiven.

THE BELIEVER'S DECLARATION OF LIBERATION©

*Thank You, Holy Spirit, for helping
me to release all control to You so that God's
Perfect Will for my life today is done.
In the Name of Jesus. Amen.*

G od can always be

trusted to do whatever He

says He will do.

—DAY—
31

THE BELIEVER'S DECLARATION OF LIBERATION©

*Thank You, Holy Spirit, for helping
me to release all control to You so that God's
Perfect Will for my life today is done.
In the Name of Jesus. Amen.*

B_e quick to ask God

for forgiveness.

DAY
1

THE BELIEVER'S DECLARATION OF LIBERATION©

*Thank You, Holy Spirit, for helping
me to release all control to You so that God's
Perfect Will for my life today is done.
In the Name of Jesus. Amen.*

God is not concerned about any ungodly things you do as long as you stop doing them.

—DAY—
2

THE BELIEVER'S DECLARATION OF LIBERATION©

*Thank You, Holy Spirit, for helping
me to release all control to You so that God's
Perfect Will for my life today is done.
In the Name of Jesus. Amen.*

Give everyone an opportunity to become a fellow believer, no matter what he or she has done.

⟶DAY⟵
3

THE BELIEVER'S DECLARATION OF LIBERATION©

*Thank You, Holy Spirit, for helping
me to release all control to You so that God's
Perfect Will for my life today is done.
In the Name of Jesus. Amen.*

Always attempt to do

more for God today than

you did yesterday.

THE BELIEVER'S DECLARATION OF LIBERATION©

*Thank You, Holy Spirit, for helping
me to release all control to You so that God's
Perfect Will for my life today is done.
In the Name of Jesus. Amen.*

Think about God all the

time and you will always

have good thoughts.

DAY
5

THE BELIEVER'S DECLARATION
OF LIBERATION©

*Thank You, Holy Spirit, for helping
me to release all control to You so that God's
Perfect Will for my life today is done.
In the Name of Jesus. Amen.*

Make it a habit of

fasting regularly.

THE BELIEVER'S DECLARATION OF LIBERATION©

*Thank You, Holy Spirit, for helping
me to release all control to You so that God's
Perfect Will for my life today is done.
In the Name of Jesus. Amen.*

Do not allow anyone to place restrictions on you when such restrictions are not found in the Bible.

DAY
7

THE BELIEVER'S DECLARATION OF LIBERATION©

*Thank You, Holy Spirit, for helping
me to release all control to You so that God's
Perfect Will for my life today is done.
In the Name of Jesus. Amen.*

Do not be influenced by religious people who insist that you not pray in the Name of Jesus.

⟶ DAY ⟵
8

THE BELIEVER'S DECLARATION OF LIBERATION©

*Thank You, Holy Spirit, for helping
me to release all control to You so that God's
Perfect Will for my life today is done.
In the Name of Jesus. Amen.*

Some people may get

upset with you when you refuse

to participate in their

"religious celebrations."

— DAY —
9

THE BELIEVER'S DECLARATION
OF LIBERATION©

*Thank You, Holy Spirit, for helping
me to release all control to You so that God's
Perfect Will for my life today is done.
In the Name of Jesus. Amen.*

Follow Jesus' example whenever you have a very important decision to make; be willing to pray all night if necessary.

DAY
10

THE BELIEVER'S DECLARATION OF LIBERATION©

*Thank You, Holy Spirit, for helping
me to release all control to You so that God's
Perfect Will for my life today is done.
In the Name of Jesus. Amen.*

W hether you pray all

night or not, always spend

quality time in prayer

seeking to hear from God.

⟶DAY⟵
11

THE BELIEVER'S DECLARATION OF LIBERATION©

*Thank You, Holy Spirit, for helping
me to release all control to You so that God's
Perfect Will for my life today is done.
In the Name of Jesus. Amen.*

Be willing to listen

whenever you have an

opportunity to hear

about Jesus.

DAY
12

THE BELIEVER'S DECLARATION OF LIBERATION©

*Thank You, Holy Spirit, for helping
me to release all control to You so that God's
Perfect Will for my life today is done.
In the Name of Jesus. Amen.*

Expect to be

healed whenever you

need healing.

⟶ DAY ⟵
13

THE BELIEVER'S DECLARATION OF LIBERATION©

*Thank You, Holy Spirit, for helping
me to release all control to You so that God's
Perfect Will for my life today is done.
In the Name of Jesus. Amen.*

Seek to develop

and maintain a good

relationship with Jesus

and do not concern

yourself with what others

may say or think

about you.

⟶ DAY ⟵
14

THE BELIEVER'S DECLARATION OF LIBERATION©

*Thank You, Holy Spirit, for helping
me to release all control to You so that God's
Perfect Will for my life today is done.
In the Name of Jesus. Amen.*

Remain focused on the things of

Jesus and let that always be your

number-one priority.

⮑DAY⮐
15

THE BELIEVER'S DECLARATION OF LIBERATION©

*Thank You, Holy Spirit, for helping
me to release all control to You so that God's
Perfect Will for my life today is done.
In the Name of Jesus. Amen.*

You should not judge or condemn others for doing the same ungodly things you have done.

~ DAY ~
16

THE BELIEVER'S DECLARATION OF LIBERATION©

*Thank You, Holy Spirit, for helping
me to release all control to You so that God's
Perfect Will for my life today is done.
In the Name of Jesus. Amen.*

Forgive others whenever

the need arises.

⟲DAY⟲
17

THE BELIEVER'S DECLARATION OF LIBERATION©

*Thank You, Holy Spirit, for helping
me to release all control to You so that God's
Perfect Will for my life today is done.
In the Name of Jesus. Amen.*

Develop the habit of reading

your Bible daily.

THE BELIEVER'S DECLARATION OF LIBERATION©

*Thank You, Holy Spirit, for helping
me to release all control to You so that God's
Perfect Will for my life today is done.
In the Name of Jesus. Amen.*

God always knows what
you have and what you
don't have.

⮞DAY⮜
19

THE BELIEVER'S DECLARATION OF LIBERATION©

*Thank You, Holy Spirit, for helping
me to release all control to You so that God's
Perfect Will for my life today is done.
In the Name of Jesus. Amen.*

Ask a mature believer

you know and respect to

help you whenever there

are sayings of Jesus you do

not understand.

THE BELIEVER'S DECLARATION OF LIBERATION©

FEB

Be prepared to believe in

Jesus permanently, not just

for a short while.

⇒ DAY ⇒
21

THE BELIEVER'S DECLARATION OF LIBERATION©

*Thank You, Holy Spirit, for helping
me to release all control to You so that God's
Perfect Will for my life today is done.
In the Name of Jesus. Amen.*

Refuse to allow the cares

and concerns of this life

to keep you from doing

God's Word consistently.

—DAY—
22

THE BELIEVER'S DECLARATION OF LIBERATION©

*Thank You, Holy Spirit, for helping
me to release all control to You so that God's
Perfect Will for my life today is done.
In the Name of Jesus. Amen.*

Always love and

respect your father and

your mother.

⤳DAY⤳
23

THE BELIEVER'S DECLARATION OF LIBERATION©

*Thank You, Holy Spirit, for helping
me to release all control to You so that God's
Perfect Will for my life today is done.
In the Name of Jesus. Amen.*

 Decide that you will always have absolute confidence in whatever Jesus says, no matter what it looks like, feels like or sounds like.

THE BELIEVER'S DECLARATION OF LIBERATION©

*Thank You, Holy Spirit, for helping
me to release all control to You so that God's
Perfect Will for my life today is done.
In the Name of Jesus. Amen.*

FEB

Do not push any panic buttons; be willing to allow the Holy Spirit to help you ride out every storm and face every challenge with confidence.

⮑ DAY ⮐
25

THE BELIEVER'S DECLARATION OF LIBERATION©

*Thank You, Holy Spirit, for helping
me to release all control to You so that God's
Perfect Will for my life today is done.
In the Name of Jesus. Amen.*

Stay in step with God

and He will be pleased to

have you in step with Him.

⟶ DAY ⟵
26

THE BELIEVER'S DECLARATION OF LIBERATION©

*Thank You, Holy Spirit, for helping
me to release all control to You so that God's
Perfect Will for my life today is done.
In the Name of Jesus. Amen.*

Give God whatever He

wants you to give Him,

and He will give you

whatever you want Him to

give you, if it agrees with

His Word.

⸻DAY⸻
27

THE BELIEVER'S DECLARATION OF LIBERATION©

*Thank You, Holy Spirit, for helping
me to release all control to You so that God's
Perfect Will for my life today is done.
In the Name of Jesus. Amen.*

Make it a habit of spending more time fellowshipping with God than you spend watching TV or on your cell phone.

DAY
28

THE BELIEVER'S DECLARATION OF LIBERATION©

*Thank You, Holy Spirit, for helping
me to release all control to You so that God's
Perfect Will for my life today is done.
In the Name of Jesus. Amen.*

When God tells you

to do anything, He expects

you to do it if you

love Him.

⟶DAY⟵
29

THE BELIEVER'S DECLARATION OF LIBERATION©

*Thank You, Holy Spirit, for helping
me to release all control to You so that God's
Perfect Will for my life today is done.
In the Name of Jesus. Amen.*

When God has blessed

you, tell somebody; it may

encourage them.

⟶DAY⟵
1

THE BELIEVER'S DECLARATION OF LIBERATION©

*Thank You, Holy Spirit, for helping
me to release all control to You so that God's
Perfect Will for my life today is done.
In the Name of Jesus. Amen.*

You do not have to do

what someone else does in

order to express your faith.

THE BELIEVER'S DECLARATION OF LIBERATION©

*Thank You, Holy Spirit, for helping
me to release all control to You so that God's
Perfect Will for my life today is done.
In the Name of Jesus. Amen.*

In most instances, it is always better that it is your faith that produces the desired results, not the faith of someone else.

DAY
3

THE BELIEVER'S DECLARATION OF LIBERATION©

*Thank You, Holy Spirit, for helping
me to release all control to You so that God's
Perfect Will for my life today is done.
In the Name of Jesus. Amen.*

There is nothing wrong with loving yourself if you save some love for others.

⮵ DAY ⮴
4

THE BELIEVER'S DECLARATION OF LIBERATION©

*Thank You, Holy Spirit, for helping
me to release all control to You so that God's
Perfect Will for my life today is done.
In the Name of Jesus. Amen.*

Rarely, if ever, is it appropriate for a single person to offer lodging to a person of the opposite sex.

DAY
5

THE BELIEVER'S DECLARATION OF LIBERATION©

*Thank You, Holy Spirit, for helping
me to release all control to You so that God's
Perfect Will for my life today is done.
In the Name of Jesus. Amen.*

Always expect to have
enough to satisfy every
need, no matter how
impossible it looks in
the natural.

⟶ DAY ⟵
6

THE BELIEVER'S DECLARATION OF LIBERATION©

*Thank You, Holy Spirit, for helping
me to release all control to You so that God's
Perfect Will for my life today is done.
In the Name of Jesus. Amen.*

Remember that as a believer, you must always do what believers do.

⟶ DAY ⟵
7

THE BELIEVER'S DECLARATION OF LIBERATION©

*Thank You, Holy Spirit, for helping
me to release all control to You so that God's
Perfect Will for my life today is done.
In the Name of Jesus. Amen.*

Do not be surprised to discover that what may appear to be too little turns out to be more than enough when God is involved.

�๏DAY๏⟩
8

THE BELIEVER'S DECLARATION OF LIBERATION©

*Thank You, Holy Spirit, for helping
me to release all control to You so that God's
Perfect Will for my life today is done.
In the Name of Jesus. Amen.*

Do not forget that Jesus' mission was to die for the sins of the world.

⇜DAY⇝
9

THE BELIEVER'S DECLARATION OF LIBERATION©

*Thank You, Holy Spirit, for helping
me to release all control to You so that God's
Perfect Will for my life today is done.
In the Name of Jesus. Amen.*

Be prepared to be

rejected the same way

Jesus was.

THE BELIEVER'S DECLARATION OF LIBERATION©

*Thank You, Holy Spirit, for helping
me to release all control to You so that God's
Perfect Will for my life today is done.
In the Name of Jesus. Amen.*

It always costs you

something if you want to

follow Jesus, but the price

is small compared to what

you gain in return.

⟶DAY⟵
11

THE BELIEVER'S DECLARATION OF LIBERATION©

*Thank You, Holy Spirit, for helping
me to release all control to You so that God's
Perfect Will for my life today is done.
In the Name of Jesus. Amen.*

It's amazing what can be accomplished when you allow the Holy Spirit to help you.

⟊DAY⟊
12

THE BELIEVER'S DECLARATION OF LIBERATION©

*Thank You, Holy Spirit, for helping
me to release all control to You so that God's
Perfect Will for my life today is done.
In the Name of Jesus. Amen.*

There will always be people who are followers of Jesus; you will not know that they are followers of Jesus.

⟞DAY⟝
13

THE BELIEVER'S DECLARATION OF LIBERATION©

*Thank You, Holy Spirit, for helping
me to release all control to You so that God's
Perfect Will for my life today is done.
In the Name of Jesus. Amen.*

Do not try to be a "lone ranger"; be willing to work with whomever God places in your life.

DAY
14

THE BELIEVER'S DECLARATION OF LIBERATION©

*Thank You, Holy Spirit, for helping
me to release all control to You so that God's
Perfect Will for my life today is done.
In the Name of Jesus. Amen.*

H elp anyone in need

whenever you are in a

position to do so.

⟞DAY⟝
15

THE BELIEVER'S DECLARATION OF LIBERATION©

Thank You, Holy Spirit, for helping me to release all control to You so that God's Perfect Will for my life today is done. In the Name of Jesus. Amen.

Before asking God for anything, spend much time praising Him by acknowledging His greatness, His goodness, and His love.

DAY
16

THE BELIEVER'S DECLARATION OF LIBERATION©

*Thank You, Holy Spirit, for helping
me to release all control to You so that God's
Perfect Will for my life today is done.
In the Name of Jesus. Amen.*

If you are not certain that

His Word promises it to

you, do not ask for it.

⮑DAY⮐
17

THE BELIEVER'S DECLARATION OF LIBERATION©

*Thank You, Holy Spirit, for helping
me to release all control to You so that God's
Perfect Will for my life today is done.
In the Name of Jesus. Amen.*

Be willing to pray

persistently, expecting to

receive whatever you are

praying for.

DAY
18

THE BELIEVER'S DECLARATION OF LIBERATION©

*Thank You, Holy Spirit, for helping
me to release all control to You so that God's
Perfect Will for my life today is done.
In the Name of Jesus. Amen.*

Expect to receive what will bless you
and not harm you when you ask God
for anything.

⮞ DAY ⮜
19

THE BELIEVER'S DECLARATION OF LIBERATION©

*Thank You, Holy Spirit, for helping
me to release all control to You so that God's
Perfect Will for my life today is done.
In the Name of Jesus. Amen.*

You cannot have it
both ways; either you
are for Jesus, or you are
against Him.

⟞DAY⟝
20

THE BELIEVER'S DECLARATION OF LIBERATION©

*Thank You, Holy Spirit, for helping
me to release all control to You so that God's
Perfect Will for my life today is done.
In the Name of Jesus. Amen.*

Accept the fact that if

Jesus is not in your life,

Satan is.

THE BELIEVER'S DECLARATION OF LIBERATION©

*Thank You, Holy Spirit, for helping
me to release all control to You so that God's
Perfect Will for my life today is done.
In the Name of Jesus. Amen.*

Realize that whenever

you have to make a choice

between family and

obeying God, choose

to obey God.

DAY
22

THE BELIEVER'S DECLARATION OF LIBERATION©

*Thank You, Holy Spirit, for helping
me to release all control to You so that God's
Perfect Will for my life today is done.
In the Name of Jesus. Amen.*

Be willing to believe in Jesus by faith
even if you never see what you think
you should see.

THE BELIEVER'S DECLARATION OF LIBERATION©

*Thank You, Holy Spirit, for helping
me to release all control to You so that God's
Perfect Will for my life today is done.
In the Name of Jesus. Amen.*

Avoid looking at or
doing anything that does
not glorify God.

─ DAY ─
24

THE BELIEVER'S DECLARATION OF LIBERATION©

*Thank You, Holy Spirit, for helping
me to release all control to You so that God's
Perfect Will for my life today is done.
In the Name of Jesus. Amen.*

Once you receive a clear understanding of the Word of God, be willing to share the Word with others as often as you have the opportunity.

⮞DAY⮜
25

THE BELIEVER'S DECLARATION OF LIBERATION©

*Thank You, Holy Spirit, for helping
me to release all control to You so that God's
Perfect Will for my life today is done.
In the Name of Jesus. Amen.*

Do not insist that you have physical proof before you believe the Word of God; always be willing to walk by faith and not by sight.

DAY
26

THE BELIEVER'S DECLARATION OF LIBERATION©

*Thank You, Holy Spirit, for helping
me to release all control to You so that God's
Perfect Will for my life today is done.
In the Name of Jesus. Amen.*

Do not knowingly

participate in any religious

ritual for which there is

not sufficient

biblical support.

～DAY～
27

THE BELIEVER'S DECLARATION OF LIBERATION©

*Thank You, Holy Spirit, for helping
me to release all control to You so that God's
Perfect Will for my life today is done.
In the Name of Jesus. Amen.*

Never think God will

not forgive you

if you repent.

DAY
28

THE BELIEVER'S DECLARATION OF LIBERATION©

*Thank You, Holy Spirit, for helping
me to release all control to You so that God's
Perfect Will for my life today is done.
In the Name of Jesus. Amen.*

Whenever you lie, you are telling God you don't trust Him enough to tell the truth.

DAY
29

THE BELIEVER'S DECLARATION OF LIBERATION©

*Thank You, Holy Spirit, for helping
me to release all control to You so that God's
Perfect Will for my life today is done.
In the Name of Jesus. Amen.*

The next time you can

pray for or with someone,

do it.

THE BELIEVER'S DECLARATION OF LIBERATION©

*Thank You, Holy Spirit, for helping
me to release all control to You so that God's
Perfect Will for my life today is done.
In the Name of Jesus. Amen.*

Never let your guard
down; resist the devil at
all times.

∽DAY∽
31

THE BELIEVER'S DECLARATION OF LIBERATION©

*Thank You, Holy Spirit, for helping
me to release all control to You so that God's
Perfect Will for my life today is done.
In the Name of Jesus. Amen.*

God has a unique

purpose for you; ask the

Holy Spirit to help you

find it.

∽DAY∽
1

THE BELIEVER'S DECLARATION OF LIBERATION©

*Thank You, Holy Spirit, for helping
me to release all control to You so that God's
Perfect Will for my life today is done.
In the Name of Jesus. Amen.*

When you are a person

of faith, you will not have

to see it before you

believe it.

DAY
2

THE BELIEVER'S DECLARATION OF LIBERATION©

*Thank You, Holy Spirit, for helping
me to release all control to You so that God's
Perfect Will for my life today is done.
In the Name of Jesus. Amen.*

Victory is yours if you

use God's Word as

your weapon.

⇌DAY⇌
3

THE BELIEVER'S DECLARATION OF LIBERATION©

*Thank You, Holy Spirit, for helping
me to release all control to You so that God's
Perfect Will for my life today is done.
In the Name of Jesus. Amen.*

Give your best to God

and He will always give

you something better.

THE BELIEVER'S DECLARATION OF LIBERATION©

*Thank You, Holy Spirit, for helping
me to release all control to You so that God's
Perfect Will for my life today is done.
In the Name of Jesus. Amen.*

God forgives you; learn to

forgive yourself.

⟂DAY⟂
5

THE BELIEVER'S DECLARATION OF LIBERATION©

*Thank You, Holy Spirit, for helping
me to release all control to You so that God's
Perfect Will for my life today is done.
In the Name of Jesus. Amen.*

When you disobey God,

you are telling Him you

don't love Him.

THE BELIEVER'S DECLARATION OF LIBERATION©

*Thank You, Holy Spirit, for helping
me to release all control to You so that God's
Perfect Will for my life today is done.
In the Name of Jesus. Amen.*

Listen to God and you

will always hear what you

need to hear.

⮕DAY⬅
7

THE BELIEVER'S DECLARATION OF LIBERATION©

*Thank You, Holy Spirit, for helping
me to release all control to You so that God's
Perfect Will for my life today is done.
In the Name of Jesus. Amen.*

Get up every

morning praising and

worshiping God.

THE BELIEVER'S DECLARATION OF LIBERATION©

*Thank You, Holy Spirit, for helping
me to release all control to You so that God's
Perfect Will for my life today is done.
In the Name of Jesus. Amen.*

There is never a time when you should say no to God and yes to yourself.

⟳DAY⟳
9

THE BELIEVER'S DECLARATION OF LIBERATION©

*Thank You, Holy Spirit, for helping
me to release all control to You so that God's
Perfect Will for my life today is done.
In the Name of Jesus. Amen.*

Doing it God's way must

always be the only way.

THE BELIEVER'S DECLARATION OF LIBERATION©

*Thank You, Holy Spirit, for helping
me to release all control to You so that God's
Perfect Will for my life today is done.
In the Name of Jesus. Amen.*

Having a plan of action
is much better than having
action without a plan.

⟞ DAY ⟝
11

THE BELIEVER'S DECLARATION OF LIBERATION©

*Thank You, Holy Spirit, for helping
me to release all control to You so that God's
Perfect Will for my life today is done.
In the Name of Jesus. Amen.*

Talking about Jesus is much better than talking about people.

THE BELIEVER'S DECLARATION OF LIBERATION©

*Thank You, Holy Spirit, for helping
me to release all control to You so that God's
Perfect Will for my life today is done.
In the Name of Jesus. Amen.*

You'll know everything

God wants you to know if

the Holy Spirit is

your teacher.

⁓DAY⁓
13

THE BELIEVER'S DECLARATION OF LIBERATION©

*Thank You, Holy Spirit, for helping
me to release all control to You so that God's
Perfect Will for my life today is done.
In the Name of Jesus. Amen.*

It's not always what you say that makes a difference; sometimes it's what you do not say that makes a difference.

THE BELIEVER'S DECLARATION OF LIBERATION©

*Thank You, Holy Spirit, for helping
me to release all control to You so that God's
Perfect Will for my life today is done.
In the Name of Jesus. Amen.*

Trying to live without Jesus in your life is like jumping out of an airplane without a parachute.

⟡DAY⟡
15

THE BELIEVER'S DECLARATION OF LIBERATION©

*Thank You, Holy Spirit, for helping
me to release all control to You so that God's
Perfect Will for my life today is done.
In the Name of Jesus. Amen.*

A wise person is someone who knows when and how to praise and glorify God.

THE BELIEVER'S DECLARATION OF LIBERATION©

*Thank You, Holy Spirit, for helping
me to release all control to You so that God's
Perfect Will for my life today is done.
In the Name of Jesus. Amen.*

Just because you are living doesn't mean that you are living the life God wants you to live.

⟶ DAY ⟶
17

THE BELIEVER'S DECLARATION OF LIBERATION©

*Thank You, Holy Spirit, for helping
me to release all control to You so that God's
Perfect Will for my life today is done.
In the Name of Jesus. Amen.*

If you do not really know

what kind of person

you are, God knows.

—DAY—
18

THE BELIEVER'S DECLARATION OF LIBERATION©

*Thank You, Holy Spirit, for helping
me to release all control to You so that God's
Perfect Will for my life today is done.
In the Name of Jesus. Amen.*

Because of the Holy Spirit, you have no excuse for not doing what God wants you to do.

⟞DAY⟝
19

THE BELIEVER'S DECLARATION OF LIBERATION©

*Thank You, Holy Spirit, for helping
me to release all control to You so that God's
Perfect Will for my life today is done.
In the Name of Jesus. Amen.*

If you want God in your life, you must first have Jesus in your life.

THE BELIEVER'S DECLARATION OF LIBERATION©

*Thank You, Holy Spirit, for helping
me to release all control to You so that God's
Perfect Will for my life today is done.
In the Name of Jesus. Amen.*

When you wake up in the morning, Jesus will be the same as He was when you went to bed.

⌒DAY⌒
21

THE BELIEVER'S DECLARATION OF LIBERATION©

*Thank You, Holy Spirit, for helping
me to release all control to You so that God's
Perfect Will for my life today is done.
In the Name of Jesus. Amen.*

When you give anything to God, you probably won't recognize it when He gives it back to you.

⟶ DAY ⟵
22

THE BELIEVER'S DECLARATION OF LIBERATION©

*Thank You, Holy Spirit, for helping
me to release all control to You so that God's
Perfect Will for my life today is done.
In the Name of Jesus. Amen.*

If God has promised you something, and you have not received it yet, keep expecting it because God does not lie.

⮜DAY⮞
23

THE BELIEVER'S DECLARATION
OF LIBERATION©

*Thank You, Holy Spirit, for helping
me to release all control to You so that God's
Perfect Will for my life today is done.
In the Name of Jesus. Amen.*

The Holy Spirit will help

you when you allow Him

to help you.

⮾DAY⮾
24

THE BELIEVER'S DECLARATION OF LIBERATION©

*Thank You, Holy Spirit, for helping
me to release all control to You so that God's
Perfect Will for my life today is done.
In the Name of Jesus. Amen.*

Although God is patient,

He does keep up with

the time.

⟶DAY⟵
25

THE BELIEVER'S DECLARATION OF LIBERATION©

*Thank You, Holy Spirit, for helping
me to release all control to You so that God's
Perfect Will for my life today is done.
In the Name of Jesus. Amen.*

God expects everyone who says

"Our Father" to act like He is.

DAY
26

THE BELIEVER'S DECLARATION OF LIBERATION©

*Thank You, Holy Spirit, for helping
me to release all control to You so that God's
Perfect Will for my life today is done.
In the Name of Jesus. Amen.*

It seems that some people

only know about God

when they are in a crisis.

⟶DAY⟵
27

THE BELIEVER'S DECLARATION OF LIBERATION©

*Thank You, Holy Spirit, for helping
me to release all control to You so that God's
Perfect Will for my life today is done.
In the Name of Jesus. Amen.*

The Holy Spirit will tell

you whatever God wants

you to do.

⊸ DAY ⊸

28

THE BELIEVER'S DECLARATION OF LIBERATION©

*Thank You, Holy Spirit, for helping
me to release all control to You so that God's
Perfect Will for my life today is done.
In the Name of Jesus. Amen.*

Jesus died for everyone,

but everyone does not

believe that He did.

DAY
29

THE BELIEVER'S DECLARATION OF LIBERATION©

*Thank You, Holy Spirit, for helping
me to release all control to You so that God's
Perfect Will for my life today is done.
In the Name of Jesus. Amen.*

The church is the people

who meet in a building

called the church.

DAY
30

THE BELIEVER'S DECLARATION OF LIBERATION©

*Thank You, Holy Spirit, for helping
me to release all control to You so that God's
Perfect Will for my life today is done.
In the Name of Jesus. Amen.*

MAY

It's always a good thing

to do when you do good

things for others.

⸺DAY⸺
1

THE BELIEVER'S DECLARATION OF LIBERATION©

*Thank You, Holy Spirit, for helping
me to release all control to You so that God's
Perfect Will for my life today is done.
In the Name of Jesus. Amen.*

Stop trying to go to

places God does not want

you to go.

$\backsim$ DAY $\backsim$
2

THE BELIEVER'S DECLARATION OF LIBERATION©

*Thank You, Holy Spirit, for helping
me to release all control to You so that God's
Perfect Will for my life today is done.
In the Name of Jesus. Amen.*

Make it a habit of giving
people what they need, not
what you don't need.

DAY
3

THE BELIEVER'S DECLARATION OF LIBERATION©

*Thank You, Holy Spirit, for helping
me to release all control to You so that God's
Perfect Will for my life today is done.
In the Name of Jesus. Amen.*

Love is the solution to

many of our problems.

THE BELIEVER'S DECLARATION OF LIBERATION©

*Thank You, Holy Spirit, for helping
me to release all control to You so that God's
Perfect Will for my life today is done.
In the Name of Jesus. Amen.*

When nothing seems to

be working, release it

to God.

⟳DAY⟳
5

THE BELIEVER'S DECLARATION OF LIBERATION©

*Thank You, Holy Spirit, for helping
me to release all control to You so that God's
Perfect Will for my life today is done.
In the Name of Jesus. Amen.*

Most of the men Jesus worked with were common ordinary men who had limited education.

THE BELIEVER'S DECLARATION OF LIBERATION©

*Thank You, Holy Spirit, for helping
me to release all control to You so that God's
Perfect Will for my life today is done.
In the Name of Jesus. Amen.*

Paul was sold out to Jesus

unlike many of

His followers.

~DAY~
7

THE BELIEVER'S DECLARATION OF LIBERATION©

*Thank You, Holy Spirit, for helping
me to release all control to You so that God's
Perfect Will for my life today is done.
In the Name of Jesus. Amen.*

Always remember

that, according to man's

standards, Jesus was

not born in the best

environment.

DAY
8

THE BELIEVER'S DECLARATION OF LIBERATION©

*Thank You, Holy Spirit, for helping
me to release all control to You so that God's
Perfect Will for my life today is done.
In the Name of Jesus. Amen.*

Some people say they believe in Jesus, but their behavior does not line up with what they say.

⟢DAY⟢
9

THE BELIEVER'S DECLARATION OF LIBERATION©

*Thank You, Holy Spirit, for helping
me to release all control to You so that God's
Perfect Will for my life today is done.
In the Name of Jesus. Amen.*

When you give God
your best, He will give you
something better.

THE BELIEVER'S DECLARATION OF LIBERATION©

*Thank You, Holy Spirit, for helping
me to release all control to You so that God's
Perfect Will for my life today is done.
In the Name of Jesus. Amen.*

The Holy Spirit is your helper whenever you are doing something God wants you to do.

⸺DAY⸺
11

THE BELIEVER'S DECLARATION OF LIBERATION©

*Thank You, Holy Spirit, for helping
me to release all control to You so that God's
Perfect Will for my life today is done.
In the Name of Jesus. Amen.*

Sometimes it is too late to

do what God tells

you to do.

⮞ DAY ⮜
12

THE BELIEVER'S DECLARATION OF LIBERATION©

*Thank You, Holy Spirit, for helping
me to release all control to You so that God's
Perfect Will for my life today is done.
In the Name of Jesus. Amen.*

Remember, everything

God says is true.

⟶DAY⟵
13

THE BELIEVER'S DECLARATION
OF LIBERATION©

*Thank You, Holy Spirit, for helping
me to release all control to You so that God's
Perfect Will for my life today is done.
In the Name of Jesus. Amen.*

Being tempted is not the sin; doing what you are tempted to do is the sin.

THE BELIEVER'S DECLARATION OF LIBERATION©

Thank You, Holy Spirit, for helping
me to release all control to You so that God's
Perfect Will for my life today is done.
In the Name of Jesus. Amen.

No one can receive your

salvation for you.

⟨DAY⟩
15

THE BELIEVER'S DECLARATION OF LIBERATION©

*Thank You, Holy Spirit, for helping
me to release all control to You so that God's
Perfect Will for my life today is done.
In the Name of Jesus. Amen.*

Evil spirits do exist

whether you believe it

or not.

THE BELIEVER'S DECLARATION OF LIBERATION©

*Thank You, Holy Spirit, for helping
me to release all control to You so that God's
Perfect Will for my life today is done.
In the Name of Jesus. Amen.*

You should believe that there is no sickness God cannot heal.

DAY
17

THE BELIEVER'S DECLARATION OF LIBERATION©

*Thank You, Holy Spirit, for helping
me to release all control to You so that God's
Perfect Will for my life today is done.
In the Name of Jesus. Amen.*

Be willing to go wherever
God intends for you to go.

18

THE BELIEVER'S DECLARATION OF LIBERATION©

*Thank You, Holy Spirit, for helping
me to release all control to You so that God's
Perfect Will for my life today is done.
In the Name of Jesus. Amen.*

Follow Jesus' example

by spending quality time

alone with God.

⟶DAY⟵
19

THE BELIEVER'S DECLARATION
OF LIBERATION©

*Thank You, Holy Spirit, for helping
me to release all control to You so that God's
Perfect Will for my life today is done.
In the Name of Jesus. Amen.*

Be willing to pay

whatever price necessary

to follow Jesus.

THE BELIEVER'S DECLARATION OF LIBERATION©

Thank You, Holy Spirit, for helping me to release all control to You so that God's Perfect Will for my life today is done. In the Name of Jesus. Amen.

Expect to be healed, no matter what you are afflicted with.

⊸DAY⊸
21

THE BELIEVER'S DECLARATION OF LIBERATION©

*Thank You, Holy Spirit, for helping
me to release all control to You so that God's
Perfect Will for my life today is done.
In the Name of Jesus. Amen.*

Be kind and someone will be

kind to you.

⟩DAY⟨
22

THE BELIEVER'S DECLARATION OF LIBERATION©

*Thank You, Holy Spirit, for helping
me to release all control to You so that God's
Perfect Will for my life today is done.
In the Name of Jesus. Amen.*

Do not be too quick to

accept all prophecies

you hear.

DAY
23

THE BELIEVER'S DECLARATION OF LIBERATION©

*Thank You, Holy Spirit, for helping
me to release all control to You so that God's
Perfect Will for my life today is done.
In the Name of Jesus. Amen.*

Jesus gave His life for
you; are you willing to give
your life for Him?

⟃DAY⟄
24

THE BELIEVER'S DECLARATION OF LIBERATION©

*Thank You, Holy Spirit, for helping
me to release all control to You so that God's
Perfect Will for my life today is done.
In the Name of Jesus. Amen.*

MAY

Don't spend too much time doing what you want to do and not enough time doing what God wants you to do.

⮞DAY⮜
25

THE BELIEVER'S DECLARATION OF LIBERATION©

*Thank You, Holy Spirit, for helping
me to release all control to You so that God's
Perfect Will for my life today is done.
In the Name of Jesus. Amen.*

If you want to be happy,

make someone happy.

DAY
26

THE BELIEVER'S DECLARATION OF LIBERATION©

*Thank You, Holy Spirit, for helping
me to release all control to You so that God's
Perfect Will for my life today is done.
In the Name of Jesus. Amen.*

Seek to always avoid getting

ahead of God.

⮞DAY⮜
27

THE BELIEVER'S DECLARATION OF LIBERATION©

*Thank You, Holy Spirit, for helping
me to release all control to You so that God's
Perfect Will for my life today is done.
In the Name of Jesus. Amen.*

B̶e willing to exercise patience while

you are waiting for God to answer

your prayers.

THE BELIEVER'S DECLARATION OF LIBERATION©

*Thank You, Holy Spirit, for helping
me to release all control to You so that God's
Perfect Will for my life today is done.
In the Name of Jesus. Amen.*

Remember, God's timing

is always perfect timing.

⟿DAY⟿
29

THE BELIEVER'S DECLARATION OF LIBERATION©

*Thank You, Holy Spirit, for helping
me to release all control to You so that God's
Perfect Will for my life today is done.
In the Name of Jesus. Amen.*

Always be prepared

because the devil is

constantly walking about

seeking whom he

can devour.

—DAY—
30

THE BELIEVER'S DECLARATION OF LIBERATION©

Thank You, Holy Spirit, for helping
me to release all control to You so that God's
Perfect Will for my life today is done.
In the Name of Jesus. Amen.

Trust God and all of

your needs will

be supplied.

⮾DAY⮾
31

THE BELIEVER'S DECLARATION
OF LIBERATION©

*Thank You, Holy Spirit, for helping
me to release all control to You so that God's
Perfect Will for my life today is done.
In the Name of Jesus. Amen.*

G od will take care of

you because He loves you

too much not to.

⮞DAY⮜
1

THE BELIEVER'S DECLARATION OF LIBERATION©

*Thank You, Holy Spirit, for helping
me to release all control to You so that God's
Perfect Will for my life today is done.
In the Name of Jesus. Amen.*

Realize that when you

reject the works of Jesus,

you are rejecting God.

—DAY—
2

THE BELIEVER'S DECLARATION OF LIBERATION©

*Thank You, Holy Spirit, for helping
me to release all control to You so that God's
Perfect Will for my life today is done.
In the Name of Jesus. Amen.*

Do not allow your lack of education to limit you from serving God.

⟍DAY⟍
3

THE BELIEVER'S DECLARATION OF LIBERATION©

*Thank You, Holy Spirit, for helping
me to release all control to You so that God's
Perfect Will for my life today is done.
In the Name of Jesus. Amen.*

Do not make the mistake of putting too much emphasis on acquiring wealth.

THE BELIEVER'S DECLARATION OF LIBERATION©

*Thank You, Holy Spirit, for helping
me to release all control to You so that God's
Perfect Will for my life today is done.
In the Name of Jesus. Amen.*

Never forget that wealth

is only a blessing when it

is used to glorify God.

DAY
5

THE BELIEVER'S DECLARATION OF LIBERATION©

*Thank You, Holy Spirit, for helping
me to release all control to You so that God's
Perfect Will for my life today is done.
In the Name of Jesus. Amen.*

Y ou can never do

too much for God.

⟨DAY⟩
6

THE BELIEVER'S DECLARATION OF LIBERATION©

*Thank You, Holy Spirit, for helping
me to release all control to You so that God's
Perfect Will for my life today is done.
In the Name of Jesus. Amen.*

Do not assume that you will enjoy the good life simply because you have wealth.

⟞DAY⟝
7

THE BELIEVER'S DECLARATION OF LIBERATION©

*Thank You, Holy Spirit, for helping
me to release all control to You so that God's
Perfect Will for my life today is done.
In the Name of Jesus. Amen.*

Money without the
right relationship with
God is always a
counterfeit blessing.

⸺DAY⸺
8

THE BELIEVER'S DECLARATION OF LIBERATION©

*Thank You, Holy Spirit, for helping
me to release all control to You so that God's
Perfect Will for my life today is done.
In the Name of Jesus. Amen.*

Time is a blessing when you use it in ways that will glorify God.

⊸ DAY ⊸
9

THE BELIEVER'S DECLARATION OF LIBERATION©

*Thank You, Holy Spirit, for helping
me to release all control to You so that God's
Perfect Will for my life today is done.
In the Name of Jesus. Amen.*

Instead of worrying, put your trust in God and do not put your trust in material things.

⮾ DAY ⮾
10

THE BELIEVER'S DECLARATION OF LIBERATION©

*Thank You, Holy Spirit, for helping
me to release all control to You so that God's
Perfect Will for my life today is done.
In the Name of Jesus. Amen.*

It's impossible to please

God without faith;

stop trying to.

⮞DAY⮜
11

THE BELIEVER'S DECLARATION OF LIBERATION©

*Thank You, Holy Spirit, for helping
me to release all control to You so that God's
Perfect Will for my life today is done.
In the Name of Jesus. Amen.*

Do not attempt to figure out when Jesus will return.

THE BELIEVER'S DECLARATION OF LIBERATION©

*Thank You, Holy Spirit, for helping
me to release all control to You so that God's
Perfect Will for my life today is done.
In the Name of Jesus. Amen.*

Expect Jesus to return

because He said that

He would.

～DAY～
13

THE BELIEVER'S DECLARATION OF LIBERATION©

*Thank You, Holy Spirit, for helping
me to release all control to You so that God's
Perfect Will for my life today is done.
In the Name of Jesus. Amen.*

Do not listen to anyone who insists that he knows when Jesus will return.

THE BELIEVER'S DECLARATION OF LIBERATION©

*Thank You, Holy Spirit, for helping
me to release all control to You so that God's
Perfect Will for my life today is done.
In the Name of Jesus. Amen.*

Jesus said only His Father

knows when He

will return.

⮞DAY⮜
15

THE BELIEVER'S DECLARATION OF LIBERATION©

*Thank You, Holy Spirit, for helping
me to release all control to You so that God's
Perfect Will for my life today is done.
In the Name of Jesus. Amen.*

Do not be surprised if you have disagreements with family members about Jesus.

THE BELIEVER'S DECLARATION OF LIBERATION©

*Thank You, Holy Spirit, for helping
me to release all control to You so that God's
Perfect Will for my life today is done.
In the Name of Jesus. Amen.*

Try to stay focused at all times on the things of God and His purpose for your life.

⟫DAY⟪
17

THE BELIEVER'S DECLARATION OF LIBERATION©

*Thank You, Holy Spirit, for helping
me to release all control to You so that God's
Perfect Will for my life today is done.
In the Name of Jesus. Amen.*

God wants you to do
whatever you can do to
resolve a dispute between
you and another person.

 DAY
18

THE BELIEVER'S DECLARATION OF LIBERATION©

*Thank You, Holy Spirit, for helping
me to release all control to You so that God's
Perfect Will for my life today is done.
In the Name of Jesus. Amen.*

Always seek to allow the

Holy Spirit to guide you.

DAY
19

THE BELIEVER'S DECLARATION OF LIBERATION©

*Thank You, Holy Spirit, for helping
me to release all control to You so that God's
Perfect Will for my life today is done.
In the Name of Jesus. Amen.*

Never allow yourself to
be bound by fear or the
traditions of men.

DAY
20

THE BELIEVER'S DECLARATION OF LIBERATION©

*Thank You, Holy Spirit, for helping
me to release all control to You so that God's
Perfect Will for my life today is done.
In the Name of Jesus. Amen.*

Do it God's way and you

will always do it the

right way.

⌒DAY⌒
21

THE BELIEVER'S DECLARATION OF LIBERATION©

*Thank You, Holy Spirit, for helping
me to release all control to You so that God's
Perfect Will for my life today is done.
In the Name of Jesus. Amen.*

B e willing to do all you

know to do in order

to enter the

Kingdom of God.

DAY
22

THE BELIEVER'S DECLARATION OF LIBERATION©

*Thank You, Holy Spirit, for helping
me to release all control to You so that God's
Perfect Will for my life today is done.
In the Name of Jesus. Amen.*

Jesus' expectations of you

do not have to agree with

your expectations of Him.

DAY
23

THE BELIEVER'S DECLARATION OF LIBERATION©

*Thank You, Holy Spirit, for helping
me to release all control to You so that God's
Perfect Will for my life today is done.
In the Name of Jesus. Amen.*

Y ou cannot have too

much faith.

THE BELIEVER'S DECLARATION OF LIBERATION©

*Thank You, Holy Spirit, for helping
me to release all control to You so that God's
Perfect Will for my life today is done.
In the Name of Jesus. Amen.*

If God says it's right,

it's right.

∽DAY∽
25

THE BELIEVER'S DECLARATION OF LIBERATION©

Thank You, Holy Spirit, for helping me to release all control to You so that God's Perfect Will for my life today is done. In the Name of Jesus. Amen.

Go where godly people are, and you will always be where God wants you to be.

⮑DAY⮐
26

THE BELIEVER'S DECLARATION OF LIBERATION©

*Thank You, Holy Spirit, for helping
me to release all control to You so that God's
Perfect Will for my life today is done.
In the Name of Jesus. Amen.*

The next time you ask God to bless you, ask Him to bless someone else first.

⮞DAY⮜
27

THE BELIEVER'S DECLARATION OF LIBERATION©

*Thank You, Holy Spirit, for helping
me to release all control to You so that God's
Perfect Will for my life today is done.
In the Name of Jesus. Amen.*

You don't have to tell God you love Him; your actions will tell Him.

DAY
28

THE BELIEVER'S DECLARATION OF LIBERATION©

*Thank You, Holy Spirit, for helping
me to release all control to You so that God's
Perfect Will for my life today is done.
In the Name of Jesus. Amen.*

If Jesus is your Lord,

God is your Father.

⮾DAY⮿
29

THE BELIEVER'S DECLARATION OF LIBERATION©

*Thank You, Holy Spirit, for helping
me to release all control to You so that God's
Perfect Will for my life today is done.
In the Name of Jesus. Amen.*

Whenever you need a miracle,

expect God to give it to you when

you ask in faith.

⮞ DAY ⮜
30

JUL

G od expects you to be a

mature follower of Jesus.

⟜DAY⟜
1

THE BELIEVER'S DECLARATION OF LIBERATION©

*Thank You, Holy Spirit, for helping
me to release all control to You so that God's
Perfect Will for my life today is done.
In the Name of Jesus. Amen.*

Your health is important
to God, and it should be
important to you.

DAY
2

THE BELIEVER'S DECLARATION OF LIBERATION©

*Thank You, Holy Spirit, for helping
me to release all control to You so that God's
Perfect Will for my life today is done.
In the Name of Jesus. Amen.*

Do not seek social status and prestigious positions for the sake of impressing people because they do not impress God.

⊸DAY⊸
3

THE BELIEVER'S DECLARATION OF LIBERATION©

*Thank You, Holy Spirit, for helping
me to release all control to You so that God's
Perfect Will for my life today is done.
In the Name of Jesus. Amen.*

Seek to walk in humility

at all times and allow God

to exalt you when

He is ready.

THE BELIEVER'S DECLARATION OF LIBERATION©

*Thank You, Holy Spirit, for helping
me to release all control to You so that God's
Perfect Will for my life today is done.
In the Name of Jesus. Amen.*

Remember, in the

Kingdom of God, service

is more important

than status.

JUL

⇌DAY⇌
5

THE BELIEVER'S DECLARATION OF LIBERATION©

*Thank You, Holy Spirit, for helping
me to release all control to You so that God's
Perfect Will for my life today is done.
In the Name of Jesus. Amen.*

Be willing to help people

who are not likely to be

able to repay you.

THE BELIEVER'S DECLARATION OF LIBERATION©

*Thank You, Holy Spirit, for helping
me to release all control to You so that God's
Perfect Will for my life today is done.
In the Name of Jesus. Amen.*

Always seek to avoid allowing the cares of this life to interfere with you keeping your commitments to God.

⸺DAY⸺
7

THE BELIEVER'S DECLARATION OF LIBERATION©

*Thank You, Holy Spirit, for helping
me to release all control to You so that God's
Perfect Will for my life today is done.
In the Name of Jesus. Amen.*

Do not put more emphasis upon seeking worldly things than on seeking godly things.

THE BELIEVER'S DECLARATION OF LIBERATION©

*Thank You, Holy Spirit, for helping
me to release all control to You so that God's
Perfect Will for my life today is done.
In the Name of Jesus. Amen.*

Remember, always seek first the Kingdom of God and all the other things of importance will automatically follow.

⟶DAY⟵
9

THE BELIEVER'S DECLARATION OF LIBERATION©

*Thank You, Holy Spirit, for helping
me to release all control to You so that God's
Perfect Will for my life today is done.
In the Name of Jesus. Amen.*

Instead of criticizing a person,

pray for him.

DAY
10

THE BELIEVER'S DECLARATION OF LIBERATION©

*Thank You, Holy Spirit, for helping
me to release all control to You so that God's
Perfect Will for my life today is done.
In the Name of Jesus. Amen.*

Nothing is more important to God than the salvation of someone who has never accepted Jesus.

$\backsim$DAY$\backsim$
11

THE BELIEVER'S DECLARATION OF LIBERATION©

Thank You, Holy Spirit, for helping me to release all control to You so that God's Perfect Will for my life today is done. In the Name of Jesus. Amen.

Never get too busy to spend time looking for a lost soul.

— DAY —
12

THE BELIEVER'S DECLARATION OF LIBERATION©

Thank You, Holy Spirit, for helping me to release all control to You so that God's Perfect Will for my life today is done. In the Name of Jesus. Amen.

Always be willing to ask for forgiveness and expect to receive it when you ask assuming you have forgiven anyone you need to forgive.

DAY 13

THE BELIEVER'S DECLARATION OF LIBERATION©

*Thank You, Holy Spirit, for helping
me to release all control to You so that God's
Perfect Will for my life today is done.
In the Name of Jesus. Amen.*

Take the focus off of
yourself and think about
the welfare of others.

⟵ DAY ⟶
14

THE BELIEVER'S DECLARATION OF LIBERATION©

*Thank You, Holy Spirit, for helping
me to release all control to You so that God's
Perfect Will for my life today is done.
In the Name of Jesus. Amen.*

Always be faithful in

whatever you attempt

to do.

DAY
15

THE BELIEVER'S DECLARATION OF LIBERATION©

Thank You, Holy Spirit, for helping me to release all control to You so that God's Perfect Will for my life today is done. In the Name of Jesus. Amen.

Never give God less

than your best.

THE BELIEVER'S DECLARATION OF LIBERATION©

*Thank You, Holy Spirit, for helping
me to release all control to You so that God's
Perfect Will for my life today is done.
In the Name of Jesus. Amen.*

Realize that faithfulness

over small things is the

best platform from which

to be given responsibilities

over more important

matters.

JUL

⟿DAY⟿
17

THE BELIEVER'S DECLARATION OF LIBERATION©

*Thank You, Holy Spirit, for helping
me to release all control to You so that God's
Perfect Will for my life today is done.
In the Name of Jesus. Amen.*

Seek to always use your money

for godly purposes.

THE BELIEVER'S DECLARATION OF LIBERATION©

*Thank You, Holy Spirit, for helping
me to release all control to You so that God's
Perfect Will for my life today is done.
In the Name of Jesus. Amen.*

Avoid any actions that

may cause you

to be dishonest.

⟿DAY⟿
19

THE BELIEVER'S DECLARATION OF LIBERATION©

*Thank You, Holy Spirit, for helping
me to release all control to You so that God's
Perfect Will for my life today is done.
In the Name of Jesus. Amen.*

Love God at all times

and you will always keep

money in its proper place.

⟨DAY⟩
20

THE BELIEVER'S DECLARATION OF LIBERATION©

*Thank You, Holy Spirit, for helping
me to release all control to You so that God's
Perfect Will for my life today is done.
In the Name of Jesus. Amen.*

D o not assume that all
so-called financial blessings are a sign
of God's blessings.

⮠DAY⮨
21

THE BELIEVER'S DECLARATION OF LIBERATION©

*Thank You, Holy Spirit, for helping
me to release all control to You so that God's
Perfect Will for my life today is done.
In the Name of Jesus. Amen.*

Recognize that there are

many people with money

who have no relationship

with God at all.

⟞DAY⟝
22

THE BELIEVER'S DECLARATION OF LIBERATION©

*Thank You, Holy Spirit, for helping
me to release all control to You so that God's
Perfect Will for my life today is done.
In the Name of Jesus. Amen.*

God does not love

anybody more than He

loves you.

⟶DAY⟵
23

THE BELIEVER'S DECLARATION OF LIBERATION©

*Thank You, Holy Spirit, for helping
me to release all control to You so that God's
Perfect Will for my life today is done.
In the Name of Jesus. Amen.*

Never seek money

for the sake of just

having money.

THE BELIEVER'S DECLARATION OF LIBERATION©

*Thank You, Holy Spirit, for helping
me to release all control to You so that God's
Perfect Will for my life today is done.
In the Name of Jesus. Amen.*

Don't expect God to
keep blessing you if you
keep disobeying Him.

� DAY ⟩
25

THE BELIEVER'S DECLARATION OF LIBERATION©

*Thank You, Holy Spirit, for helping
me to release all control to You so that God's
Perfect Will for my life today is done.
In the Name of Jesus. Amen.*

Do not knowingly cause

anyone to sin.

THE BELIEVER'S DECLARATION OF LIBERATION©

*Thank You, Holy Spirit, for helping
me to release all control to You so that God's
Perfect Will for my life today is done.
In the Name of Jesus. Amen.*

Accept Jesus early in life

and you will have more

time to serve Him.

≈DAY≈
27

THE BELIEVER'S DECLARATION OF LIBERATION©

*Thank You, Holy Spirit, for helping
me to release all control to You so that God's
Perfect Will for my life today is done.
In the Name of Jesus. Amen.*

Give God all you have,

and He will give you more

than you will ever

give Him.

THE BELIEVER'S DECLARATION
OF LIBERATION©

*Thank You, Holy Spirit, for helping
me to release all control to You so that God's
Perfect Will for my life today is done.
In the Name of Jesus. Amen.*

The good news is that there is no other God but the God Who has a Son named Jesus.

⇜DAY⇝
29

THE BELIEVER'S DECLARATION OF LIBERATION©

Thank You, Holy Spirit, for helping me to release all control to You so that God's Perfect Will for my life today is done. In the Name of Jesus. Amen.

Bless yourself by becoming a tither, if you are not already one.

THE BELIEVER'S DECLARATION OF LIBERATION©

*Thank You, Holy Spirit, for helping
me to release all control to You so that God's
Perfect Will for my life today is done.
In the Name of Jesus. Amen.*

God loves you and He

knows you love Him when

you obey Him.

�20DAY�
31

THE BELIEVER'S DECLARATION OF LIBERATION©

*Thank You, Holy Spirit, for helping
me to release all control to You so that God's
Perfect Will for my life today is done.
In the Name of Jesus. Amen.*

B e especially careful
not to say or do anything
that may mislead a person
who has very limited
knowledge about the
things of God.

⟳DAY⟳
1

THE BELIEVER'S DECLARATION OF LIBERATION©

*Thank You, Holy Spirit, for helping
me to release all control to You so that God's
Perfect Will for my life today is done.
In the Name of Jesus. Amen.*

Faithfulness is godliness,

and both are God pleasers.

⟡DAY⟡
2

THE BELIEVER'S DECLARATION OF LIBERATION©

*Thank You, Holy Spirit, for helping
me to release all control to You so that God's
Perfect Will for my life today is done.
In the Name of Jesus. Amen.*

Always do what God

requires you to do because

He expects you to.

⤳DAY⤳
3

THE BELIEVER'S DECLARATION OF LIBERATION©

*Thank You, Holy Spirit, for helping
me to release all control to You so that God's
Perfect Will for my life today is done.
In the Name of Jesus. Amen.*

Never be hesitant to ask God to have mercy on you, and always expect to receive what you ask for.

⟞DAY⟝
4

THE BELIEVER'S DECLARATION OF LIBERATION©

*Thank You, Holy Spirit, for helping
me to release all control to You so that God's
Perfect Will for my life today is done.
In the Name of Jesus. Amen.*

Y̲ou can have anything

you want if what you want

is what God wants

you to have.

AUG

THE BELIEVER'S DECLARATION OF LIBERATION©

*Thank You, Holy Spirit, for helping
me to release all control to You so that God's
Perfect Will for my life today is done.
In the Name of Jesus. Amen.*

Thank God first for what He has

done for you before asking Him

to do more for you.

⟶ DAY ⟵
6

THE BELIEVER'S DECLARATION OF LIBERATION©

*Thank You, Holy Spirit, for helping
me to release all control to You so that God's
Perfect Will for my life today is done.
In the Name of Jesus. Amen.*

Remember to thank those who have helped you, no matter how small the help is.

AUG

⟿DAY⟿
7

THE BELIEVER'S DECLARATION OF LIBERATION©

Thank You, Holy Spirit, for helping me to release all control to You so that God's Perfect Will for my life today is done. In the Name of Jesus. Amen.

Do not miss any opportunity to get and keep your life in order and be ready whenever the Kingdom of God appears in its fullness.

THE BELIEVER'S DECLARATION OF LIBERATION©

*Thank You, Holy Spirit, for helping
me to release all control to You so that God's
Perfect Will for my life today is done.
In the Name of Jesus. Amen.*

Always thank God for your earthly possessions, but never become so attached to them that you forget who gave them to you.

AUG

⟞DAY⟝
9

THE BELIEVER'S DECLARATION OF LIBERATION©

*Thank You, Holy Spirit, for helping
me to release all control to You so that God's
Perfect Will for my life today is done.
In the Name of Jesus. Amen.*

Before saying no to

someone, pray about it;

God may want you

to say yes.

⌒DAY⌒
10

THE BELIEVER'S DECLARATION OF LIBERATION©

*Thank You, Holy Spirit, for helping
me to release all control to You so that God's
Perfect Will for my life today is done.
In the Name of Jesus. Amen.*

All children are very

important to Jesus.

DAY
11

THE BELIEVER'S DECLARATION OF LIBERATION©

Thank You, Holy Spirit, for helping me to release all control to You so that God's Perfect Will for my life today is done. In the Name of Jesus. Amen.

Remain humble and full of joy as you anticipate entering the Kingdom of God.

⮞ DAY ⮜
12

THE BELIEVER'S DECLARATION OF LIBERATION©

*Thank You, Holy Spirit, for helping
me to release all control to You so that God's
Perfect Will for my life today is done.
In the Name of Jesus. Amen.*

Be willing to give up

wealth, anything, or

anyone in order to

follow Jesus.

AUG

⟞DAY⟝
13

THE BELIEVER'S DECLARATION OF LIBERATION©

Thank You, Holy Spirit, for helping me to release all control to You so that God's Perfect Will for my life today is done. In the Name of Jesus. Amen.

If you have wealth, don't assume that you don't need God.

THE BELIEVER'S DECLARATION OF LIBERATION©

*Thank You, Holy Spirit, for helping
me to release all control to You so that God's
Perfect Will for my life today is done.
In the Name of Jesus. Amen.*

Money does not have

to get in the way of your

salvation if you are willing

to keep it in its

proper place.

⟳DAY⟳
15

THE BELIEVER'S DECLARATION OF LIBERATION©

*Thank You, Holy Spirit, for helping
me to release all control to You so that God's
Perfect Will for my life today is done.
In the Name of Jesus. Amen.*

Accept by faith that the

Holy Spirit will help you

to resolve all of

your problems.

⟿ DAY ⟿
16

THE BELIEVER'S DECLARATION OF LIBERATION©

*Thank You, Holy Spirit, for helping
me to release all control to You so that God's
Perfect Will for my life today is done.
In the Name of Jesus. Amen.*

W henever you need

healing or need a miracle,

have faith that you can

and will receive what

you need.

~DAY~
17

THE BELIEVER'S DECLARATION OF LIBERATION©

*Thank You, Holy Spirit, for helping
me to release all control to You so that God's
Perfect Will for my life today is done.
In the Name of Jesus. Amen.*

When you pray,

expect God to answer

your prayer.

⟶ DAY ⟵
18

THE BELIEVER'S DECLARATION OF LIBERATION©

*Thank You, Holy Spirit, for helping
me to release all control to You so that God's
Perfect Will for my life today is done.
In the Name of Jesus. Amen.*

Be willing to associate

with anyone you believe

you may be instrumental

in getting to accept Jesus.

⮞DAY⮜
19

AUG

THE BELIEVER'S DECLARATION OF LIBERATION©

Thank You, Holy Spirit, for helping me to release all control to You so that God's Perfect Will for my life today is done. In the Name of Jesus. Amen.

God is always pleased when you do your best and give your best whenever you have the opportunity.

⮞DAY⮜
20

THE BELIEVER'S DECLARATION
OF LIBERATION©

*Thank You, Holy Spirit, for helping
me to release all control to You so that God's
Perfect Will for my life today is done.
In the Name of Jesus. Amen.*

Remember, you

can and should always do

something that

glorifies God.

⟩DAY⟨
21

THE BELIEVER'S DECLARATION OF LIBERATION©

Thank You, Holy Spirit, for helping me to release all control to You so that God's Perfect Will for my life today is done. In the Name of Jesus. Amen.

D̲o not expect Jesus to be anyone other than who the Bible says He is.

─DAY─
22

THE BELIEVER'S DECLARATION OF LIBERATION©

*Thank You, Holy Spirit, for helping
me to release all control to You so that God's
Perfect Will for my life today is done.
In the Name of Jesus. Amen.*

B e willing to always be a

person of peace.

⌐DAY⌐
23

THE BELIEVER'S DECLARATION OF LIBERATION©

*Thank You, Holy Spirit, for helping
me to release all control to You so that God's
Perfect Will for my life today is done.
In the Name of Jesus. Amen.*

Remember, the

peacemakers are the ones

who are called the

sons of God.

~ DAY ~
24

THE BELIEVER'S DECLARATION OF LIBERATION©

*Thank You, Holy Spirit, for helping
me to release all control to You so that God's
Perfect Will for my life today is done.
In the Name of Jesus. Amen.*

P ray constantly that

everyone you know will

accept Jesus.

AUG

⮑ DAY ⮒
25

THE BELIEVER'S DECLARATION OF LIBERATION©

*Thank You, Holy Spirit, for helping
me to release all control to You so that God's
Perfect Will for my life today is done.
In the Name of Jesus. Amen.*

Accept the fact that Jesus

came to seek and save

those who were lost.

DAY
26

THE BELIEVER'S DECLARATION OF LIBERATION©

*Thank You, Holy Spirit, for helping
me to release all control to You so that God's
Perfect Will for my life today is done.
In the Name of Jesus. Amen.*

Do not make it a habit of questioning the authority of Jesus or those who speak on His behalf.

⟶DAY⟵
27

THE BELIEVER'S DECLARATION OF LIBERATION©

*Thank You, Holy Spirit, for helping
me to release all control to You so that God's
Perfect Will for my life today is done.
In the Name of Jesus, Amen.*

Y ou don't always need
to pray to hear from God;
read your Bible.

THE BELIEVER'S DECLARATION OF LIBERATION©

*Thank You, Holy Spirit, for helping
me to release all control to You so that God's
Perfect Will for my life today is done.
In the Name of Jesus. Amen.*

D o not ever forget that Jesus, the Anointed One, was killed because He represented God and not the traditions of men.

AUG

⬧DAY⬧
29

THE BELIEVER'S DECLARATION OF LIBERATION©

*Thank You, Holy Spirit, for helping
me to release all control to You so that God's
Perfect Will for my life today is done.
In the Name of Jesus. Amen.*

It should always be either

God's way or no way.

THE BELIEVER'S DECLARATION OF LIBERATION©

*Thank You, Holy Spirit, for helping
me to release all control to You so that God's
Perfect Will for my life today is done.
In the Name of Jesus. Amen.*

Believe in the

resurrection even though

you may not completely

understand it.

AUG

⬤DAY⬤
31

THE BELIEVER'S DECLARATION OF LIBERATION©

*Thank You, Holy Spirit, for helping
me to release all control to You so that God's
Perfect Will for my life today is done.
In the Name of Jesus. Amen.*

Remember, wherever you go you are taking the Holy Spirit with you; don't ever forget this.

SEP

⮞DAY⮜
1

THE BELIEVER'S DECLARATION OF LIBERATION©

*Thank You, Holy Spirit, for helping
me to release all control to You so that God's
Perfect Will for my life today is done.
In the Name of Jesus. Amen.*

Do not be taken in by people who profess to be godly, but their behavior does not support what they profess.

⟞DAY⟝
2

THE BELIEVER'S DECLARATION OF LIBERATION©

*Thank You, Holy Spirit, for helping
me to release all control to You so that God's
Perfect Will for my life today is done.
In the Name of Jesus. Amen.*

If you know that you won't do it, don't say you will, because God hates a liar.

⟁DAY⟁
3

THE BELIEVER'S DECLARATION OF LIBERATION©

*Thank You, Holy Spirit, for helping
me to release all control to You so that God's
Perfect Will for my life today is done.
In the Name of Jesus. Amen.*

Do not become afraid
of anything that happens
on earth or in the heavens
because none of these
events will keep Jesus
from returning.

DAY
4

THE BELIEVER'S DECLARATION OF LIBERATION©

*Thank You, Holy Spirit, for helping
me to release all control to You so that God's
Perfect Will for my life today is done.
In the Name of Jesus. Amen.*

E xpect Jesus to return at

any time and remain ready

at all times.

SEP

⟞DAY⟝
5

THE BELIEVER'S DECLARATION OF LIBERATION©

*Thank You, Holy Spirit, for helping
me to release all control to You so that God's
Perfect Will for my life today is done.
In the Name of Jesus. Amen.*

Always celebrate Holy
Communion and other
celebrations that are part
of the Christian tradition
and are supported by
the Bible.

DAY
6

THE BELIEVER'S DECLARATION OF LIBERATION©

Thank You, Holy Spirit, for helping me to release all control to You so that God's Perfect Will for my life today is done. In the Name of Jesus. Amen.

Be willing to be tolerant of other believers' views; focus on the essentials.

SEP

⟩DAY⟨
7

THE BELIEVER'S DECLARATION OF LIBERATION©

*Thank You, Holy Spirit, for helping
me to release all control to You so that God's
Perfect Will for my life today is done.
In the Name of Jesus. Amen.*

If you want to have an

important job, be one of

God's servants.

THE BELIEVER'S DECLARATION OF LIBERATION©

*Thank You, Holy Spirit, for helping
me to release all control to You so that God's
Perfect Will for my life today is done.
In the Name of Jesus. Amen.*

When your emphasis

is on how much and how

often you can serve others,

you will not have to seek

greatness; greatness will

find you.

SEP

⮞DAY⮜
9

THE BELIEVER'S DECLARATION OF LIBERATION©

*Thank You, Holy Spirit, for helping
me to release all control to You so that God's
Perfect Will for my life today is done.
In the Name of Jesus. Amen.*

Expect Satan to attempt to destroy

you, but expect to be rescued by

the Holy Spirit.

DAY
10

THE BELIEVER'S DECLARATION OF LIBERATION©

*Thank You, Holy Spirit, for helping
me to release all control to You so that God's
Perfect Will for my life today is done.
In the Name of Jesus. Amen.*

N ever be afraid to tell

anyone that you

know Jesus.

⌒DAY⌒
11

THE BELIEVER'S DECLARATION OF LIBERATION©

Thank You, Holy Spirit, for helping me to release all control to You so that God's Perfect Will for my life today is done. In the Name of Jesus. Amen.

Do your best to say "not my will, but Your will be done" whenever you are faced with not wanting to do what God wants you to do.

DAY
12

THE BELIEVER'S DECLARATION OF LIBERATION©

*Thank You, Holy Spirit, for helping
me to release all control to You so that God's
Perfect Will for my life today is done.
In the Name of Jesus. Amen.*

D o not allow your enemies to cause you to show anything other than love whenever you have the opportunity to do so.

⤳DAY⤳
13

THE BELIEVER'S DECLARATION OF LIBERATION©

*Thank You, Holy Spirit, for helping
me to release all control to You so that God's
Perfect Will for my life today is done.
In the Name of Jesus. Amen.*

Do not be surprised that whenever you confront religious traditions and powers, you may be persecuted.

—DAY—
14

THE BELIEVER'S DECLARATION OF LIBERATION©

*Thank You, Holy Spirit, for helping
me to release all control to You so that God's
Perfect Will for my life today is done.
In the Name of Jesus. Amen.*

Never stoop to the level
of those who falsely accuse
you; always remain the
godly person you must be.

SEP

⌒DAY⌒
15

THE BELIEVER'S DECLARATION OF LIBERATION©

*Thank You, Holy Spirit, for helping
me to release all control to You so that God's
Perfect Will for my life today is done.
In the Name of Jesus. Amen.*

Strong leaders do not

allow weak and evil people

to influence them to

do evil; instead, strong

leaders influence weak

people to do good.

⟶ DAY ⟶
16

THE BELIEVER'S DECLARATION OF LIBERATION©

*Thank You, Holy Spirit, for helping
me to release all control to You so that God's
Perfect Will for my life today is done.
In the Name of Jesus. Amen.*

One of the worst lies

you can tell is when you lie

to yourself.

SEP

—DAY—
17

THE BELIEVER'S DECLARATION OF LIBERATION©

*Thank You, Holy Spirit, for helping
me to release all control to You so that God's
Perfect Will for my life today is done.
In the Name of Jesus. Amen.*

Be willing to exercise

self-control at all times.

THE BELIEVER'S DECLARATION OF LIBERATION©

*Thank You, Holy Spirit, for helping
me to release all control to You so that God's
Perfect Will for my life today is done.
In the Name of Jesus. Amen.*

Learn to say "no" to self and

"yes" to Jesus.

⟳DAY⟳
19

THE BELIEVER'S DECLARATION OF LIBERATION©

*Thank You, Holy Spirit, for helping
me to release all control to You so that God's
Perfect Will for my life today is done.
In the Name of Jesus. Amen.*

N ever be guilty of rejecting

or disrespecting Jesus or those

who represent Him.

⟶DAY⟵
20

THE BELIEVER'S DECLARATION OF LIBERATION©

*Thank You, Holy Spirit, for helping
me to release all control to You so that God's
Perfect Will for my life today is done.
In the Name of Jesus. Amen.*

Because of your relationship with Jesus, your sins are forgiven, and you can come to God on your own behalf anytime you wish to do so.

SEP

⟵DAY⟶
21

THE BELIEVER'S DECLARATION OF LIBERATION©

*Thank You, Holy Spirit, for helping
me to release all control to You so that God's
Perfect Will for my life today is done.
In the Name of Jesus. Amen.*

Always seek to do what you can do
for God and do not focus on what
you cannot do.

THE BELIEVER'S DECLARATION OF LIBERATION©

*Thank You, Holy Spirit, for helping
me to release all control to You so that God's
Perfect Will for my life today is done.
In the Name of Jesus. Amen.*

Always believe what

Jesus says.

∽DAY∽
23

THE BELIEVER'S DECLARATION OF LIBERATION©

*Thank You, Holy Spirit, for helping
me to release all control to You so that God's
Perfect Will for my life today is done.
In the Name of Jesus. Amen.*

Jesus never said anything that is not true and that has not or will not be a manifested truth.

⟶DAY⟵
24

Y ou cannot earn love

because if it has to be

earned, it's not love.

SEP

⌁DAY⌁
25

THE BELIEVER'S DECLARATION OF LIBERATION©

*Thank You, Holy Spirit, for helping
me to release all control to You so that God's
Perfect Will for my life today is done.
In the Name of Jesus. Amen.*

B̲e prepared to pass

any test that you may

encounter; never accuse

God of tempting you.

⟶ DAY ⟵
26

THE BELIEVER'S DECLARATION OF LIBERATION©

*Thank You, Holy Spirit, for helping
me to release all control to You so that God's
Perfect Will for my life today is done.
In the Name of Jesus. Amen.*

Accept the fact that whenever you sin, you do so because you want to, not because someone or something forced you to sin.

SEP

⌒DAY⌒
27

THE BELIEVER'S DECLARATION OF LIBERATION©

*Thank You, Holy Spirit, for helping
me to release all control to You so that God's
Perfect Will for my life today is done.
In the Name of Jesus. Amen.*

B e thankful that

everything God gives you

is good and perfect.

⟿ DAY ⟿
28

THE BELIEVER'S DECLARATION OF LIBERATION©

*Thank You, Holy Spirit, for helping
me to release all control to You so that God's
Perfect Will for my life today is done.
In the Name of Jesus. Amen.*

Every chance you get, express

your gratitude that you do not have

to convince God that you deserve

whatever He does for you.

SEP

⟿DAY⟾
29

THE BELIEVER'S DECLARATION OF LIBERATION©

*Thank You, Holy Spirit, for helping
me to release all control to You so that God's
Perfect Will for my life today is done.
In the Name of Jesus. Amen.*

Be glad to be one of

God's servants, realizing

that there is no

greater title.

⮜DAY⮞
30

THE BELIEVER'S DECLARATION OF LIBERATION©

Thank You, Holy Spirit, for helping me to release all control to You so that God's Perfect Will for my life today is done. In the Name of Jesus. Amen.

God expects you to love yourself, but He also expects you to love others.

OCT

～DAY～
1

THE BELIEVER'S DECLARATION OF LIBERATION©

*Thank You, Holy Spirit, for helping
me to release all control to You so that God's
Perfect Will for my life today is done.
In the Name of Jesus. Amen.*

Forgive yourself because

God has.

⌒DAY⌒
2

THE BELIEVER'S DECLARATION OF LIBERATION©

*Thank You, Holy Spirit, for helping
me to release all control to You so that God's
Perfect Will for my life today is done.
In the Name of Jesus. Amen.*

Don't stop believing

in God when you cannot

have your way.

OCT

⟶DAY⟵
3

THE BELIEVER'S DECLARATION OF LIBERATION©

*Thank You, Holy Spirit, for helping
me to release all control to You so that God's
Perfect Will for my life today is done.
In the Name of Jesus. Amen.*

Your prayers will be

answered if they

are answerable.

DAY
4

THE BELIEVER'S DECLARATION OF LIBERATION©

*Thank You, Holy Spirit, for helping
me to release all control to You so that God's
Perfect Will for my life today is done.
In the Name of Jesus. Amen.*

When you accept Jesus
as your Savior, you have
made the most important
decision you will
ever make.

OCT

⟞DAY⟝
5

THE BELIEVER'S DECLARATION OF LIBERATION©

Thank You, Holy Spirit, for helping me to release all control to You so that God's Perfect Will for my life today is done. In the Name of Jesus. Amen.

When you start listening to the Holy Spirit, you will become the winner God created you to be.

DAY
6

THE BELIEVER'S DECLARATION OF LIBERATION©

*Thank You, Holy Spirit, for helping
me to release all control to You so that God's
Perfect Will for my life today is done.
In the Name of Jesus. Amen.*

G od is not displeased

with you because you

make mistakes when you

are trying to do His will.

OCT

⟨⟩DAY⟨⟩
7

THE BELIEVER'S DECLARATION OF LIBERATION©

*Thank You, Holy Spirit, for helping
me to release all control to You so that God's
Perfect Will for my life today is done.
In the Name of Jesus. Amen.*

Getting angry is not

ungodly; it's staying angry

that is ungodly.

THE BELIEVER'S DECLARATION OF LIBERATION©

*Thank You, Holy Spirit, for helping
me to release all control to You so that God's
Perfect Will for my life today is done.
In the Name of Jesus. Amen.*

O nly the Holy Spirit

can help you

forgive and forget.

OCT

⊸DAY⊸
9

THE BELIEVER'S DECLARATION OF LIBERATION©

*Thank You, Holy Spirit, for helping
me to release all control to You so that God's
Perfect Will for my life today is done.
In the Name of Jesus. Amen.*

Before you disobey God,

think about who you

are disobeying.

THE BELIEVER'S DECLARATION OF LIBERATION©

*Thank You, Holy Spirit, for helping
me to release all control to You so that God's
Perfect Will for my life today is done.
In the Name of Jesus. Amen.*

D o not be afraid to love Jesus and

have faith in Him, although

you have not seen Him.

OCT

 DAY
11

THE BELIEVER'S DECLARATION OF LIBERATION©

*Thank You, Holy Spirit, for helping
me to release all control to You so that God's
Perfect Will for my life today is done.
In the Name of Jesus. Amen.*

Thank God daily for allowing you

to know about salvation and how

it can be received.

THE BELIEVER'S DECLARATION OF LIBERATION©

*Thank You, Holy Spirit, for helping
me to release all control to You so that God's
Perfect Will for my life today is done.
In the Name of Jesus. Amen.*

Rejoice in knowing that all your loved ones can receive salvation, if they believe in Jesus Christ.

OCT

$\sim$DAY$\sim$
13

THE BELIEVER'S DECLARATION OF LIBERATION©

Thank You, Holy Spirit, for helping me to release all control to You so that God's Perfect Will for my life today is done. In the Name of Jesus. Amen.

You must learn who the Holy Spirit is and what He does.

⇐ DAY ⇒
14

THE BELIEVER'S DECLARATION
OF LIBERATION©

*Thank You, Holy Spirit, for helping
me to release all control to You so that God's
Perfect Will for my life today is done.
In the Name of Jesus. Amen.*

A̶sk the Holy Spirit

to help you pray only

answerable prayers.

~DAY~
15

THE BELIEVER'S DECLARATION OF LIBERATION©

Thank You, Holy Spirit, for helping me to release all control to You so that God's Perfect Will for my life today is done. In the Name of Jesus. Amen.

D o not forget that you are expected to spread the gospel every day wherever you are.

⟳ DAY ⟳
16

THE BELIEVER'S DECLARATION OF LIBERATION©

*Thank You, Holy Spirit, for helping
me to release all control to You so that God's
Perfect Will for my life today is done.
In the Name of Jesus. Amen.*

B̲e willing to give back to

God some of what He has

given you.

OCT

⮾DAY⮾
17

THE BELIEVER'S DECLARATION OF LIBERATION©

*Thank You, Holy Spirit, for helping
me to release all control to You so that God's
Perfect Will for my life today is done.
In the Name of Jesus. Amen.*

Ask the Holy Spirit to teach you

how to exercise self-control in all

areas of your life.

THE BELIEVER'S DECLARATION
OF LIBERATION©

*Thank You, Holy Spirit, for helping
me to release all control to You so that God's
Perfect Will for my life today is done.
In the Name of Jesus. Amen.*

Always believe that

God's love for you is

greater than your sin.

DAY
19

THE BELIEVER'S DECLARATION OF LIBERATION©

*Thank You, Holy Spirit, for helping
me to release all control to You so that God's
Perfect Will for my life today is done.
In the Name of Jesus. Amen.*

Never forget that it was Jesus' obedience that caused Him to be willing to die and offer His blood to God for your sins.

THE BELIEVER'S DECLARATION OF LIBERATION©

*Thank You, Holy Spirit, for helping
me to release all control to You so that God's
Perfect Will for my life today is done.
In the Name of Jesus. Amen.*

Choose to believe that

men and women of all ages

continue to believe in God

because of what Jesus did.

OCT

◦DAY◦
21

THE BELIEVER'S DECLARATION OF LIBERATION©

*Thank You, Holy Spirit, for helping
me to release all control to You so that God's
Perfect Will for my life today is done.
In the Name of Jesus. Amen.*

Have unconditional love for others because God has unconditional love for you.

⮂ DAY ⮀
22

THE BELIEVER'S DECLARATION OF LIBERATION©

*Thank You, Holy Spirit, for helping
me to release all control to You so that God's
Perfect Will for my life today is done.
In the Name of Jesus. Amen.*

Do not forget it is your

love for others that tells

them you are

a real Christian.

~DAY~
23

THE BELIEVER'S DECLARATION OF LIBERATION©

*Thank You, Holy Spirit, for helping
me to release all control to You so that God's
Perfect Will for my life today is done.
In the Name of Jesus. Amen.*

Y ou can love

unconditionally if you will

allow the Holy Spirit to

help you.

⟞ DAY ⟝
24

THE BELIEVER'S DECLARATION OF LIBERATION©

*Thank You, Holy Spirit, for helping
me to release all control to You so that God's
Perfect Will for my life today is done.
In the Name of Jesus. Amen.*

Everyone who wants to

be born again will if they

are willing to do it

God's way.

OCT

∽DAY∽
25

THE BELIEVER'S DECLARATION OF LIBERATION©

*Thank You, Holy Spirit, for helping
me to release all control to You so that God's
Perfect Will for my life today is done.
In the Name of Jesus. Amen.*

Do not make the

mistake of believing that

you are someone you

are not.

THE BELIEVER'S DECLARATION OF LIBERATION©

*Thank You, Holy Spirit, for helping
me to release all control to You so that God's
Perfect Will for my life today is done.
In the Name of Jesus. Amen.*

Do what God's Word
says and you will live with
Him forever.

~DAY~
27

THE BELIEVER'S DECLARATION OF LIBERATION©

*Thank You, Holy Spirit, for helping
me to release all control to You so that God's
Perfect Will for my life today is done.
In the Name of Jesus. Amen.*

Ask the Holy Spirit

to help you remove all

ungodliness from your life.

DAY
28

THE BELIEVER'S DECLARATION OF LIBERATION©

*Thank You, Holy Spirit, for helping
me to release all control to You so that God's
Perfect Will for my life today is done.
In the Name of Jesus. Amen.*

Never lose sight of

the fact that you are

only passing through

this world; it is not your

permanent home.

⇜DAY⇝
29

THE BELIEVER'S DECLARATION OF LIBERATION©

*Thank You, Holy Spirit, for helping
me to release all control to You so that God's
Perfect Will for my life today is done.
In the Name of Jesus. Amen.*

Trying to act like a
Christian doesn't make
you a Christian.

THE BELIEVER'S DECLARATION OF LIBERATION©

*Thank You, Holy Spirit, for helping
me to release all control to You so that God's
Perfect Will for my life today is done.
In the Name of Jesus. Amen.*

Jesus wants every born-again believer to be the church rather than going to church.

OCT

❧DAY❧
31

THE BELIEVER'S DECLARATION OF LIBERATION©

*Thank You, Holy Spirit, for helping
me to release all control to You so that God's
Perfect Will for my life today is done.
In the Name of Jesus. Amen.*

As a believer, you must seek to become a godly role model who other believers can copy.

NOV

∽DAY∽
1

THE BELIEVER'S DECLARATION OF LIBERATION©

*Thank You, Holy Spirit, for helping
me to release all control to You so that God's
Perfect Will for my life today is done.
In the Name of Jesus. Amen.*

Whenever you disobey

the "laws of the land,"

be willing to suffer the

consequences of

your actions.

⟶ DAY ⟵
2

THE BELIEVER'S DECLARATION OF LIBERATION©

*Thank You, Holy Spirit, for helping
me to release all control to You so that God's
Perfect Will for my life today is done.
In the Name of Jesus. Amen.*

Applaud those who

are courageous enough

to disobey man's laws in

order to obey God's laws.

NOV

⟋DAY⟍
3

THE BELIEVER'S DECLARATION OF LIBERATION©

*Thank You, Holy Spirit, for helping
me to release all control to You so that God's
Perfect Will for my life today is done.
In the Name of Jesus. Amen.*

Do not expect preferential treatment from your employer because he is a fellow believer.

THE BELIEVER'S DECLARATION OF LIBERATION©

*Thank You, Holy Spirit, for helping
me to release all control to You so that God's
Perfect Will for my life today is done.
In the Name of Jesus. Amen.*

As a Christian wife, do not preach to your unbelieving husband; let God change his heart.

∽DAY∽
5

THE BELIEVER'S DECLARATION OF LIBERATION©

*Thank You, Holy Spirit, for helping
me to release all control to You so that God's
Perfect Will for my life today is done.
In the Name of Jesus. Amen.*

Wives, do not forget that when you disrespect your husbands, you disrespect God.

DAY
6

THE BELIEVER'S DECLARATION OF LIBERATION©

*Thank You, Holy Spirit, for helping
me to release all control to You so that God's
Perfect Will for my life today is done.
In the Name of Jesus. Amen.*

Christian wives, do not focus too much on your outward appearance; put your greatest emphasis on your godly character.

NOV

⤙DAY⤚
7

THE BELIEVER'S DECLARATION OF LIBERATION©

*Thank You, Holy Spirit, for helping
me to release all control to You so that God's
Perfect Will for my life today is done.
In the Name of Jesus. Amen.*

Christian husbands,

treat your wives right if

you want your

prayers answered.

DAY
8

THE BELIEVER'S DECLARATION OF LIBERATION©

*Thank You, Holy Spirit, for helping
me to release all control to You so that God's
Perfect Will for my life today is done.
In the Name of Jesus. Amen.*

Christian husbands
and wives, remember that
whatever either of you
receives, it must be shared
equally with each other.

⌒DAY⌒
9

THE BELIEVER'S DECLARATION OF LIBERATION©

*Thank You, Holy Spirit, for helping
me to release all control to You so that God's
Perfect Will for my life today is done.
In the Name of Jesus. Amen.*

Seek to be a person of

unity, and always speak

well of others.

THE BELIEVER'S DECLARATION
OF LIBERATION©

*Thank You, Holy Spirit, for helping
me to release all control to You so that God's
Perfect Will for my life today is done.
In the Name of Jesus. Amen.*

Be quick to show
compassion to others and
to love everyone.

NOV

⮾DAY⮾
11

THE BELIEVER'S DECLARATION OF LIBERATION©

*Thank You, Holy Spirit, for helping
me to release all control to You so that God's
Perfect Will for my life today is done.
In the Name of Jesus. Amen.*

Having a humble spirit

is always pleasing to God.

THE BELIEVER'S DECLARATION OF LIBERATION©

*Thank You, Holy Spirit, for helping
me to release all control to You so that God's
Perfect Will for my life today is done.
In the Name of Jesus. Amen.*

Never repay evil with evil; always respond to evil with good.

DAY
13

THE BELIEVER'S DECLARATION OF LIBERATION©

*Thank You, Holy Spirit, for helping
me to release all control to You so that God's
Perfect Will for my life today is done.
In the Name of Jesus. Amen.*

Do not allow your

tongue to speak evil

of anyone.

⟶ DAY ⟵
14

THE BELIEVER'S DECLARATION OF LIBERATION©

*Thank You, Holy Spirit, for helping
me to release all control to You so that God's
Perfect Will for my life today is done.
In the Name of Jesus. Amen.*

With the help of the Holy Spirit, you will be the person God created you to be.

∽DAY∽
15

NOV

THE BELIEVER'S DECLARATION OF LIBERATION©

*Thank You, Holy Spirit, for helping
me to release all control to You so that God's
Perfect Will for my life today is done.
In the Name of Jesus. Amen.*

All believers must do
the will of God all the
time no matter how much
suffering they
must endure.

⮾ DAY ⮾
16

THE BELIEVER'S DECLARATION OF LIBERATION©

*Thank You, Holy Spirit, for helping
me to release all control to You so that God's
Perfect Will for my life today is done.
In the Name of Jesus. Amen.*

J esus must be the

number-one role model

for every Christian.

DAY
17

THE BELIEVER'S DECLARATION OF LIBERATION©

*Thank You, Holy Spirit, for helping
me to release all control to You so that God's
Perfect Will for my life today is done.
In the Name of Jesus. Amen.*

Always remember that

you are saved because of

God's grace and mercy, not

because of your goodness.

⟶ DAY ⟵
18

THE BELIEVER'S DECLARATION OF LIBERATION©

*Thank You, Holy Spirit, for helping
me to release all control to You so that God's
Perfect Will for my life today is done.
In the Name of Jesus. Amen.*

Thinking about Jesus

is the best thinking you'll

ever do.

NOV

∽DAY∽
19

THE BELIEVER'S DECLARATION OF LIBERATION©

*Thank You, Holy Spirit, for helping
me to release all control to You so that God's
Perfect Will for my life today is done.
In the Name of Jesus. Amen.*

Don't say it if you
wouldn't say it if you knew
God was listening.

THE BELIEVER'S DECLARATION OF LIBERATION©

*Thank You, Holy Spirit, for helping
me to release all control to You so that God's
Perfect Will for my life today is done.
In the Name of Jesus. Amen.*

D o not allow yourself
to be controlled by pride
because a prideful person
displeases God greatly.

NOV

⟿DAY⟿
21

THE BELIEVER'S DECLARATION OF LIBERATION©

*Thank You, Holy Spirit, for helping
me to release all control to You so that God's
Perfect Will for my life today is done.
In the Name of Jesus. Amen.*

Spend as much time as possible studying the Word of God, not just reading the Word.

~ DAY ~
22

THE BELIEVER'S DECLARATION OF LIBERATION©

*Thank You, Holy Spirit, for helping
me to release all control to You so that God's
Perfect Will for my life today is done.
In the Name of Jesus. Amen.*

If you are victimized by false teachers and false teaching, you will never know and enjoy all of the blessings God has for you.

NOV

DAY
23

THE BELIEVER'S DECLARATION OF LIBERATION©

*Thank You, Holy Spirit, for helping
me to release all control to You so that God's
Perfect Will for my life today is done.
In the Name of Jesus. Amen.*

Always give God your
best and everything He
gives you will always be
His best because
everything He does is
always His best.

⌁DAY⌁
24

THE BELIEVER'S DECLARATION OF LIBERATION©

*Thank You, Holy Spirit, for helping
me to release all control to You so that God's
Perfect Will for my life today is done.
In the Name of Jesus. Amen.*

Make it your business to

know false teaching when

you hear it.

∽DAY∽
25

THE BELIEVER'S DECLARATION OF LIBERATION©

*Thank You, Holy Spirit, for helping
me to release all control to You so that God's
Perfect Will for my life today is done.
In the Name of Jesus. Amen.*

Y ou cannot know God

unless you know

His Word.

DAY
26

THE BELIEVER'S DECLARATION OF LIBERATION©

*Thank You, Holy Spirit, for helping
me to release all control to You so that God's
Perfect Will for my life today is done.
In the Name of Jesus. Amen.*

You must release all
control to the Holy Spirit
to receive His help.

⟶DAY⟵
27

THE BELIEVER'S DECLARATION OF LIBERATION©

*Thank You, Holy Spirit, for helping
me to release all control to You so that God's
Perfect Will for my life today is done.
In the Name of Jesus. Amen.*

Remember, it is the Holy Spirit who produces the fruit of the Spirit.

THE BELIEVER'S DECLARATION OF LIBERATION©

*Thank You, Holy Spirit, for helping
me to release all control to You so that God's
Perfect Will for my life today is done.
In the Name of Jesus. Amen.*

Study the Word of God

so you will not be a victim

of false teachers.

DAY
29

THE BELIEVER'S DECLARATION OF LIBERATION©

*Thank You, Holy Spirit, for helping
me to release all control to You so that God's
Perfect Will for my life today is done.
In the Name of Jesus. Amen.*

Stick with God and He will

stick with you.

DAY
30

THE BELIEVER'S DECLARATION OF LIBERATION©

*Thank You, Holy Spirit, for helping
me to release all control to You so that God's
Perfect Will for my life today is done.
In the Name of Jesus. Amen.*

Refuse to spend

your life being a

"part-time" Christian.

⊸DAY⊸
1

DEC

THE BELIEVER'S DECLARATION OF LIBERATION©

*Thank You, Holy Spirit, for helping
me to release all control to You so that God's
Perfect Will for my life today is done.
In the Name of Jesus. Amen.*

W here you spend the

rest of your life is a choice

you make in this life.

⸻ DAY ⸻
2

THE BELIEVER'S DECLARATION OF LIBERATION©

Thank You, Holy Spirit, for helping me to release all control to You so that God's Perfect Will for my life today is done. In the Name of Jesus. Amen.

Nothing happens

without God knowing

about it before it happens.

⮑DAY⮐
3

THE BELIEVER'S DECLARATION OF LIBERATION©

*Thank You, Holy Spirit, for helping
me to release all control to You so that God's
Perfect Will for my life today is done.
In the Name of Jesus. Amen.*

G od will not allow ungodliness

to go on forever.

⮞DAY⮜
4

THE BELIEVER'S DECLARATION OF LIBERATION©

*Thank You, Holy Spirit, for helping
me to release all control to You so that God's
Perfect Will for my life today is done.
In the Name of Jesus. Amen.*

God is always aware of evil

and evildoers.

━DAY━
5

THE BELIEVER'S DECLARATION OF LIBERATION©

*Thank You, Holy Spirit, for helping
me to release all control to You so that God's
Perfect Will for my life today is done.
In the Name of Jesus. Amen.*

Get it the right way and

you will always enjoy it the

right way.

DAY
6

THE BELIEVER'S DECLARATION OF LIBERATION©

*Thank You, Holy Spirit, for helping
me to release all control to You so that God's
Perfect Will for my life today is done.
In the Name of Jesus. Amen.*

When you don't know, ask the Holy Spirit to help you identify false teachers and their false teachings.

⟶DAY⟵
7

DEC

THE BELIEVER'S DECLARATION OF LIBERATION©

*Thank You, Holy Spirit, for helping
me to release all control to You so that God's
Perfect Will for my life today is done.
In the Name of Jesus. Amen.*

When you do what God
tells you to do, He will do
what He tells you
He will do.

⟬ DAY ⟭
8

A good man is good

because he is a man

of God.

⟿ DAY ⟿
9

THE BELIEVER'S DECLARATION OF LIBERATION©

*Thank You, Holy Spirit, for helping
me to release all control to You so that God's
Perfect Will for my life today is done.
In the Name of Jesus. Amen.*

Never forget that you

are one of God's children

because Jesus is your Lord.

—DAY—
10

THE BELIEVER'S DECLARATION OF LIBERATION©

*Thank You, Holy Spirit, for helping
me to release all control to You so that God's
Perfect Will for my life today is done.
In the Name of Jesus. Amen.*

God loves you 24/7 no matter

what you do.

⟶ DAY ⟶
11

THE BELIEVER'S DECLARATION OF LIBERATION©

*Thank You, Holy Spirit, for helping
me to release all control to You so that God's
Perfect Will for my life today is done.
In the Name of Jesus. Amen.*

As one of His children,

you must live your life in

a manner that will always

bring glory to God.

� DAY 653
12

THE BELIEVER'S DECLARATION OF LIBERATION©

Thank You, Holy Spirit, for helping me to release all control to You so that God's Perfect Will for my life today is done. In the Name of Jesus. Amen.

There will always be certain people who you must stay away from.

THE BELIEVER'S DECLARATION OF LIBERATION©

*Thank You, Holy Spirit, for helping
me to release all control to You so that God's
Perfect Will for my life today is done.
In the Name of Jesus. Amen.*

Look forward to seeing

Jesus either here or

in Heaven.

—DAY—
14

THE BELIEVER'S DECLARATION OF LIBERATION©

*Thank You, Holy Spirit, for helping
me to release all control to You so that God's
Perfect Will for my life today is done.
In the Name of Jesus. Amen.*

Put forth every effort
possible to live a godly life.

THE BELIEVER'S DECLARATION OF LIBERATION©

*Thank You, Holy Spirit, for helping
me to release all control to You so that God's
Perfect Will for my life today is done.
In the Name of Jesus. Amen.*

God expects you to love

everyone even people who

make it almost impossible

to love them.

THE BELIEVER'S DECLARATION OF LIBERATION©

*Thank You, Holy Spirit, for helping
me to release all control to You so that God's
Perfect Will for my life today is done.
In the Name of Jesus. Amen.*

Give God what you
promised to give Him, and
He will give you what He
promised to give you.

$\backsim$DAY$\backsim$
17

DEC

THE BELIEVER'S DECLARATION OF LIBERATION©

Thank You, Holy Spirit, for helping me to release all control to You so that God's Perfect Will for my life today is done. In the Name of Jesus. Amen.

God will disapprove

of you if you keep doing

things He disapproves of.

⌒DAY⌒
18

THE BELIEVER'S DECLARATION OF LIBERATION©

*Thank You, Holy Spirit, for helping
me to release all control to You so that God's
Perfect Will for my life today is done.
In the Name of Jesus. Amen.*

A full-time Christian

will not become a

practicing sinner again.

◦DAY◦
19

DEC

THE BELIEVER'S DECLARATION OF LIBERATION©

*Thank You, Holy Spirit, for helping
me to release all control to You so that God's
Perfect Will for my life today is done.
In the Name of Jesus. Amen.*

There are some things

you must not expect God

to give you.

⮡ DAY ⮠
20

THE BELIEVER'S DECLARATION OF LIBERATION©

*Thank You, Holy Spirit, for helping
me to release all control to You so that God's
Perfect Will for my life today is done.
In the Name of Jesus. Amen.*

Love everything

God loves.

THE BELIEVER'S DECLARATION OF LIBERATION©

Thank You, Holy Spirit, for helping me to release all control to You so that God's Perfect Will for my life today is done. In the Name of Jesus. Amen.

Don't ever trust the devil because he is not trustworthy.

~DAY~
22

THE BELIEVER'S DECLARATION OF LIBERATION©

*Thank You, Holy Spirit, for helping
me to release all control to You so that God's
Perfect Will for my life today is done.
In the Name of Jesus. Amen.*

Decide that you will

always live your life like

you are a child of God.

∼DAY∼
23

THE BELIEVER'S DECLARATION OF LIBERATION©

*Thank You, Holy Spirit, for helping
me to release all control to You so that God's
Perfect Will for my life today is done.
In the Name of Jesus. Amen.*

Never forget the fact

that you must consistently

exhibit brotherly love if

you want to be known as a

person who is committed

to living for God.

⮜DAY⮞
24

THE BELIEVER'S DECLARATION OF LIBERATION©

*Thank You, Holy Spirit, for helping
me to release all control to You so that God's
Perfect Will for my life today is done.
In the Name of Jesus. Amen.*

K now that some of the people

of the world will hate you the same

as they hated Jesus.

≈DAY≈
25

THE BELIEVER'S DECLARATION OF LIBERATION©

*Thank You, Holy Spirit, for helping
me to release all control to You so that God's
Perfect Will for my life today is done.
In the Name of Jesus. Amen.*

Never allow yourself to become a
hater nor have anger, bitterness or
contempt for anyone.

DAY
26

THE BELIEVER'S DECLARATION OF LIBERATION©

*Thank You, Holy Spirit, for helping
me to release all control to You so that God's
Perfect Will for my life today is done.
In the Name of Jesus. Amen.*

Learn to listen to the

Holy Spirit when He talks

to you.

⮑DAY⮐
27

DEC

THE BELIEVER'S DECLARATION OF LIBERATION©

*Thank You, Holy Spirit, for helping
me to release all control to You so that God's
Perfect Will for my life today is done.
In the Name of Jesus. Amen.*

Remember, God always
existed and He always will.

THE BELIEVER'S DECLARATION OF LIBERATION©

*Thank You, Holy Spirit, for helping
me to release all control to You so that God's
Perfect Will for my life today is done.
In the Name of Jesus. Amen.*

Don't give anything to
anyone you would not like
to receive.

⮞DAY⮜
29

DEC

THE BELIEVER'S DECLARATION OF LIBERATION©

*Thank You, Holy Spirit, for helping
me to release all control to You so that God's
Perfect Will for my life today is done.
In the Name of Jesus. Amen.*

It's always time to do

things the way God wants

them to be done.

‿DAY‿
30

THE BELIEVER'S DECLARATION OF LIBERATION©

Thank You, Holy Spirit, for helping me to release all control to You so that God's Perfect Will for my life today is done. In the Name of Jesus. Amen.

Thank God for allowing you to see the end of another year; tell Him that this was a great year, but you believe next year will be greater.

⇌ DAY ⇌
31

DEC